Dear White Women, It's Not You. It's Me. I'm Breaking Up With You!

Commentaries on Race, White Feminism, Allyship and Intersectionality

HANNAH L. DRAKE

Drake Publishing

D1165157

Dear White Women, It's Not You. It's Me. I'm
Breaking Up With You!
Commentaries on Race, White Feminism, Allyship
and Intersectionality

Copyright ©2019 by Hannah L. Drake
Published by Drake Publishing
ISBN-13: 978-0-9972992-2-9
ISBN-10: 0-9972992-2-3
Printed in the United States of America.

Author Photo: Jessie Kriech-Higdon
Kriech-HigdonPhotography

Inside Author Photo: Lola Honey
lolahoney.glossgenius.com

—

Dedicated to…

Those who are willing to read, to listen, to pay the dues.

"I would be a liar, a hypocrite, or a fool - and I'm not any of those - to say that I don't write for the reader. I do. But for the reader who hears, who really will work at it, going behind what I seem to say. So I write for myself and that reader who will pay the dues."
– Maya Angelou

—

Table of Contents

—

Table of Contents

—

Introduction

Perhaps you picked up this book up because you have read my other work, you enjoy my poetry, you have heard me speak. Maybe you picked it up because you liked the title, or perhaps you picked up because you genuinely desire to have more understanding about Racism, White Feminism, Allyship, and Intersectionality. It is all intertwined. Whatever your reason(s), I am glad that you chose to read through these pages.

I am opening this book with *The 10 Stages of Facing Racism* because it is essential for you to see yourself and face yourself, then read the remainder of this book. It will be easy to, "Not All," "Not Me," your way out of the reality of this book. I challenge you to not take the easy way out.

Dear White Women, It's Not You. It's Me. I'm Breaking Up With You! will not be an easy read for many people, but when have I ever written anything that is easy?

Challenge yourself to read through it and come out on the other side.

With Love & Revolution,
Hannah

THE 10 STAGES OF FACING RACISM

As a Black woman dealing with racism, I remember I used to get so upset trying to speak to White people about racism. Why couldn't they just understand? It all seemed so simple to me. As I observed people and had many conversations, both online and in-person, I started to see similar patterns of behavior when it came to facing racism. In thinking about racism, I was reminded of the Five Stages of Grief (Denial, Anger, Bargaining, Depression, Acceptance) developed by David Kessler and Elisabeth Kübler-Ross. I realized that facing racism has a similar process. There are stages of facing the reality of racism.

Before you read any further, let me be clear, these are the stages of facing racism that I have noticed in my personal and professional life. To be sure, there are others and this list is not exhaustive but hopefully will provide some understanding about Facing Racism in America.

10 Stages of Facing Racism:

1.   **Denial**- The first stage of racism is Denial. Instead of facing the truth that racism is and has been a persistent problem in the United States, it is easier to deny that racism exists. Denial means making tweets that say, "This isn't us," when in fact, history shows that it is you. America was built on the backs of enslaved Black men, women, and children. In the wake of two mass shootings perpetrated by two White men in recent days, the

conversation of White supremacy started to surface. Tucker Carlson stated on his Fox News show, "If you were to assemble a list, a hierarchy of concerns, problems this country has, where would white supremacy be on the list? Right up there with Russia probably. It's actually not a real problem in America." Tucker, like many other White people, are in denial. Countless historical and current events dispute Tucker's claim, yet he, like many others, have chosen to be willfully ignorant. They have chosen to remain in denial.

I recall reading a study (and I am sorry that I cannot find it to cite it) that people can only look at themselves for a few seconds in the mirror before turning away. I believe the study said it was just 15 seconds before someone will look away from their own reflection. It is difficult to look at yourself physically because our minds immediately start pointing out what we perceive are "flaws." Similarly, it is even harder to look inside yourself, see yourself, and admit the truth about yourself-all the ugly parts that you dress up so no one can see them. Facing your inner self is painful. It doesn't feel good. It is uncomfortable. And like anyone that feels discomfort, the first thing you want to do is try to alleviate the discomfort. Most people do that with denial. "This isn't happening." "Our President isn't racist." "America isn't racist." "It's not me that is racist. You're the real racist." People say things like this because admitting the truth says a lot about them and their families and their friends. It means everything they have ever believed about themselves, and this country is a lie. It means their husbands and daughters and church members and neighbors, etc., supported a racist, and how can that be? "What does that say about me? So, I must deny that racism even exists."

2.   **Avoidance** – The second stage of racism is Avoidance. "I unfollowed Hannah. All she does is talk about race." "I'm blocking you on social media." "Don't come over for dinner if all you are going to do is talk about race." This phase is similar to denial, except the person can't entirely deny that what you are saying bears some truth. Instead of facing the reality of racism, they would rather avoid the conversation. They would like to pretend as if they do not know anything about racism. How many times have you heard, "Why do you keep talking about racism?" "Just stop talking about race, and it will go away." "Talking about racism just makes it more prevalent." Talking about an issue does not cause an issue, it brings awareness to an issue, and that is the part that many White people want to avoid because it makes them accountable. If they know about racism, they can no longer rest in the denial phase. They can no longer claim, "I had no idea." They can no longer rest in their ignorance. And if we are honest, some people are comfortable going to bed every night oblivious to anything going on around them. It makes it easier to sleep at night in your

king-size bed with Egyptian cotton sheets when you don't have to think about kids being locked in cages sleeping on a floor.

3.   **Anger**– The third stage of racism is Anger. By this phase, White people can longer deny or avoid the reality that racism exists yet they still do not want to face it, so they become angry. "How dare you question the President and call him racist!" "Go back to where you came from!" "Racist bitch!" It is easier to respond in anger than it is facing the truth. Anger allows them to have a villain, and that makes racism acceptable. It's not racism. It's Colin Kaepernick. He's the villain." "It's not racism. It's Representative Ilhan Omar. She's the villain." "It's not racism. It's those immigrants coming to steal our jobs. They are the villains." "It's not racism. It's liberal Hollywood. The elite. They are the villains."

Donald J. Trump ✔ @realDonaldTr... · 16m
Liberal Hollywood is Racist at the highest level, and with great Anger and Hate! They like to call themselves "Elite," but they are not Elite. In fact, it is often the people that they so strongly oppose that are actually the Elite. The movie coming out is made in order....

Donald J. Trump ✔
@realDonaldTrump

....to inflame and cause chaos. They create their own violence, and then try to blame others. They are the true Racists, and are very bad for our Country!

White people who are not ready to face racism will find a person(s) to point to in order to make racism justifiable to them. Then it stops being about racism and starts being about the person(s). The villain is the source of the problem so that can now justify racist behavior. It is like, "I wouldn't behave this way, but they made me do it. They made me lash out." Their anger is really a reflection of their refusal to look inside themselves and instead of facing inwardly to deal with themselves, they turn their anger outwardly.

4.   **Deflection** – The fourth stage of racism is Deflection. I like to call this phase the, "But What About" phase. White people can no longer deny racism exists; they can no longer avoid the conversation about racism, but because they do not want to face the truth, it is time for deflection.   Ivanka Trump demonstrated this phase after the mass shootings in El Paso, Texas, and Dayton, Ohio. The world started to call her father, Donald Trump, out on his racism, and she could no longer deny that her father has stoked the flames of hatred in America. The videos of his racist rhetoric were talking points on almost every news station, in the newspapers, and saturated social media so she could not avoid the truth. So, it was time for her to deflect. In typical fashion, she chose not to address her father but shine a spotlight on Chicago the go-to city for anyone that really wants to say, "But what about Black on Black crime?" Deflection merely means the person still does not want to face the reality of racism. They can no longer deny that racism exists, but they are not ready to deal with that knowledge so

they must deflect. It also helps them accept the actions of racism.

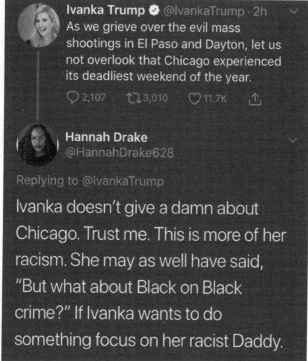

> **Ivanka Trump** ✔ @IvankaTrump · 2h
> As we grieve over the evil mass shootings in El Paso and Dayton, let us not overlook that Chicago experienced its deadliest weekend of the year.
>
> 💬 2,107   🔁 3,010   ♡ 11.7K   ⬆
>
> **Hannah Drake**
> @HannahDrake628
>
> Replying to @IvankaTrump
>
> Ivanka doesn't give a damn about Chicago. Trust me. This is more of her racism. She may as well have said, "But what about Black on Black crime?" If Ivanka wants to do something focus on her racist Daddy.

5.   **Victimhood** – The fifth stage of racism is Victimhood. At this stage, the evidence of racism is overwhelming. They can no longer deny, avoid, get angry or deflect. So now it becomes about them being the victim. "White people are oppressed too." "Irish people were enslaved too." "I feel threatened." "Your tone when you speak about racism makes me uncomfortable."   "I feel attacked." "We are the real victims." This is a phase that seeks to take the focus off the injustices

that Black people face and now make it about White people. If they cannot deny that racism exists, now they must make themselves the victim. If any sympathy is going to be given, it must be given towards them. Enter White tears. They work every time. This is yet another tactic that helps them avoid facing racism.

6.   **Separation** – The sixth stage of racism is Separation. White people can no longer deny, avoid, deflect, or play the victim, so to now it becomes about separating. When I make an argument about police brutality, inevitably someone will come on my posts and say, "Not all police are bad." So now they have dismissed my argument and made it about all police. No one said all police are bad. But they don't want to deal with the reality that police are killing unarmed Black people. When I write about the 53% of White women that voted for Trump, a White woman will always say, "Not all White women." No one said all White women, but they must make it known that they are not like "those women." (I think it is common sense when someone makes a statement they don't mean EVERY anything in the world but that goes back to stage 4, Deflection. Instead of listening to the argument they deflect to separation to make sure they are not grouped in with "those people.") They are not like "those White men," with tiki torches spewing hate in Charlottesville, Virginia. They are different. They aren't in the group of people that are tearing

young children away from their parents and locking them up in cages. They are different. They are separate from "those White people." They are the "good White people." "I'm not like Trump. I would have voted for Obama a third time if I could have." What they fail to understand is that racism doesn't start or end with one person. Trump didn't invent racism. He just used what was already there for his benefit. Racism is embedded into systems all White people benefit from regardless if they are racist or not. There is no parsing out racism. Fighting racism means admitting even if you are not racist, you have benefitted from racist systems. But they do not want to admit that so they must separate themselves as if that absolves them from facing and dealing with racism.

7. **Rationalizing** – The seventh stage of racism is Rationalizing. Somehow White people must make racism make sense, so they start to rationalize. I like to call this phase the, "If they would just..." phase. "If they would just pull up their pants then..." "If they would just stop playing their music loudly then..." "If they would just comply then..." When you do not want to admit something, you start using anything to rationalize it away. White people believe if Black people would just stay in their place, all would be well. If Black people would just conform to what White people want, racism wouldn't exist. They have formed a quid pro quo rationalization, but there is no quid pro quo when it comes to racism. There is

no "if Black people would just _____
(fill in the blank) then" because Black people are
criminalized, penalized, and murdered for doing
almost anything. We have seen countless videos in
recent months of Black people being harassed for
walking, barbecuing, swimming, driving, etc. The
list is endless. You cannot rationalize away racism.

8.   **Depression**– The eighth stage of racism is
Depression. By this phase, White people
understand they cannot deny, avoid, get angry,
deflect, play the victim, separate themselves, or
rationalize away racism. The reality of racism is
sinking in, and it doesn't feel good.   This is the
current phase America is in after the mass
shootings that took place in El Paso, Texas, and
Dayton, Ohio. America is realizing that indeed,
America is racist, and that realization has caused
some to be depressed. "I can't believe this is
happening." "I'm so sad." "Who have we
become?" "I 'can't eat. I can't sleep." Still, this is a
phase that is about them. They are still centering
themselves. The attention is not on those that have
experienced racism; it is about how this realization
has made them feel. If they are depressed since
Trump has been elected, imagine how Black
people have felt every single day since before the
Presidential election? The feelings of sadness,
hopelessness, and despair are nothing new for us.
We wake up with those feelings, go throughout
our day with those feelings, and go to bed with
those feelings.

9.   **Acceptance** – The ninth stage of racism is Acceptance. This is the phase I am waiting for America to reach. There is no more denying that racism is real. There is no more denying that racism is embedded in just about every system in America. There is no more denying that America elected a racist into the highest office in the land. The evidence is clear. This nation was built on racism, and this nation continues to feed off the undying fruit of racism. It is time for America to stop dealing with the fruit and deal with the root. Now it is time to accept this painful reality. You cannot deny or rationalize it away. It simply is. Facing this truth and owning this truth is difficult for many, but until you are able to get to this phase, change will not take place. Dealing with racism means accepting that racism exists. It means accepting that yes, your father was a racist. It means acknowledging that your family wealth was gained due to slavery. It means you are in your position not because you were better qualified but because the other applicant was Black and the hiring manager didn't like Black people. It means acknowledging some ugly and hidden truths about yourself that are difficult to admit. But only through admitting and accepting them can you begin to change.

10.   **Action** – The final stage of facing racism is Action. I like to call this phase, "So Now What?" Now that you have admitted that racism is real, now what? What do you do with this

reality? Now isn't the time to sit and do nothing. Do something! Stand up. Speak out. Advocate for others. Donate your time. Give resources. Attend a local meeting that focuses on race relations. Read. Educate yourself. Equip yourself to speak to those that are where you once were when it comes to facing racism. Get comfortable being uncomfortable. Check yourself. Understand that people are in different phases of facing racism. Listen. Don't assume because you now understand that racism is, in fact, real, that you are the spokesperson for race relations. Some people have been in this fight for justice for a long time. Listen to them and learn from them.

Understanding these 10 stages of racism have helped me maintain my composure when I speak to people about racism. (Most times. I'm not perfect.) I used to get so upset when people would deflect or lash out in anger. Now I understand there are stages they must go through in order to get to accepting and facing racism. My job as a writer is to continue to hold up the mirror until they see themselves, face themselves, and are ready to accept the truth.

DEAR AMERICA: YOU SHOULD HAVE LISTENED. SINCERELY, A BLACK WOMAN

Everything you need to save this nation can be found in a Black woman. The mother of all civilization and creation. Black women are the epitome of grace under pressure, resilience, power, love and strength. Black women have always been at the forefront of a movement, under-girding a movement for liberation.

It was Harriet Tubman that reminded us how to deal with oppressors, "Never wound a snake, Kill it."

It was Ellen Craft, a slave, that used her privilege to pass to free herself and her husband and declared, "I have never had the slightest inclination whatever of returning to bondage."

It was Mamie Till, who allowed the world to see the horror of racism by allowing an open casket funeral for her son, Emmett Till.

It was Coretta Scott King that displayed silent strength as she sat veiled at her husband's funeral, poised and stoic as her daughter rested her head in her lap and knew that she would have to continue the fight for Civil Rights even though being in the fight made her a widow.

It was Betty Shabazz that showed the love of a mother as she grabbed her children and pushed them to the floor beneath a bench shielding them with her body as her husband Malcolm was assassinated.

It was Sojourner Truth that was a one-woman feminist movement declaring, "If the first woman God ever made was strong enough to turn the world upside down all alone, these women together ought to be able to turn it back, and get it right side up again!"

It was Phillis Wheatley that reminded us, "In every human beast, God has implanted a principle, which we call love of freedom; it is impatient of oppression, and pants for deliverance."

It was Fannie Lou Hamer that told us, "Nobody is free until everybody is free." She stood boldly in the face of injustice and said, "I guess if I'd had any sense, I'd have been a little scared – but what was the point of being scared? The only thing they could do was kill me, and it kinda seemed like they'd been trying to do that a little bit at a time since I could remember."

It was Diane Nash that reminded us that we are the leaders that we have been searching for. "Freedom, by definition, is people realizing that they are their own leaders."

It was Jo-Ann Robinson that was social media before social media was social media who created flyers to organize support for the Montgomery Bus Boycotts in 1955.

It was Assata Shakur that reminded us, "It is our duty to fight for our freedom. It is our duty to win. We much love each other and support each other. We have nothing to lose but our chains!"

Black women have always stood on the front lines and the sidelines. We have endured humiliation and embarrassment. We have stood naked on auction blocks and watched the world pick our bodies apart and put them on display. We were shamed for our appearance as this world made

White women the standard for beauty, yet White men snuck into our quarters to rape us. We were humiliated for our skin color, lips and hip size yet this world built an empire trying to imitate what we were given naturally. We were subjected to playing wet nurse to your babies when we couldn't even be there for our own. We were the conductor on the railroad to freedom. We fried the chicken, made the cornbread and packed the lunches for marches so our people could have nourishment. We ironed the shirts and pressed the pants, kept a clean home and cooked dinner in between fighting off the KKK. We made the signs and provided slogans that would change the world. We sat at the counters all while they spit in our faces and poured milkshakes over our heads. We endured the bites of dogs and hits from billy clubs. We assisted this nation in exploring the universe yet couldn't even use the restroom in the very building we worked. We started movements that shook a nation. We stood backstage as the world demanded a man be center stage garnering credit for a movement. We buried our sons and our daughters too soon. We endured medical malpractice as the medical community used our bodies for Frankenstein research. We became the face of a movement fueled by our children's blood. We were pioneers for freedom. We stood up to the system. We organized. We prayed. We fought. We resisted. We sang songs that encouraged our people to rise up, to speak out, to stand up. We warned you, America that this day would indeed be coming because chickens always come home to roost. Do not ask us to console you during this time. We are no longer your wet nurse, your mammy, your maid. Your head will no longer rest in our bosom. For years we have listened to the cries of our ancestors from just beneath the soil, we have watched our husbands swaying in the trees, we have buried our daughters and wept as our sons were gunned down in the street. Daily, in this world, we rest on a bed of despair, we awaken to false hope. We screamed for justice and you turned a deaf ear and blind eye to our plight. Do not call us because you now wonder about your sense of security, something we have never known. We do not have the time or the inclination to be concerned about your tears. Because even as we wept, no one was ever concerned about ours. This time, you must weep alone. We resign ourselves from being the shoulder that you need to cry on. Find your own hope. Search for it deeply. I suggest, looking in the mirror first. Perhaps there you will find the reason that you now weep. And when you see your reflection, look beyond yourself and see the pain, suffering, and

acts of horror that have been inflicted on people that did you no harm, that wanted nothing from you, that just wanted the basic right to simply be human and to be left alone.

So perhaps where America should start is making right everything that it has done wrong. Until then, I stand on the words of Ms. Celie, who said, "Until you do right by me, everything you even think about gonna fail!"

Sincerely,

A Black Woman

NOW IS NOT THE TIME FOR WHITE TEARS

Dear White People,

In the wake of the Philando Castile verdict, now is the not the time for White tears. Now is not the time to ask Black people, "What can we do?" Now is not the time to ask Black people to console you, to make you feel better, to absolve you of your guilt.

While I know that many White people woke up Wednesday, November 9, 2016, and realized that America is still ripe with injustice, greed, corruption, and racism, this is something that Black people have always known because we live it every day. Our history in America begins with tragedy and suffering and continues daily. While I know, you have marched, made protest signs, read Ta-Nehisi Coates, listened to Kendrick and got in Formation with Beyonce; you will never understand the deep-rooted, gut-wrenching agony of defeat and pain we feel, almost collectively, when yet another officer walks free after they murder a Black person.

These names are not just catchy hashtags for us to toss on Twitter or Facebook to make us feel like we are a part of the revolution.

For every loss of life due to the hands of a police officer or a renegade neighborhood patrol, we mourn. We mourn the lives of people who we will never know but that we know can easily be us. People that look like our mothers, fathers, aunts, uncles, sons, daughters and friends. Justice for us is buried in an unmarked grave.

We weep because we know in this world we will never be safe. We weep because we know our children are not safe. That driving for us can have life or death consequences. That wearing a hoodie can be our death sentence. That a simple trip to the store for Skittles and tea can lead to our families picking out caskets. We know that driving while Black is criminalistic, that walking while Black can be deadly. That breathing while Black has been known to cause death. We live in a world that doesn't value our lives. That never valued our humanity, That never saw our humanity. That will murder us in the street like a dog and charge us for the bullets. That will hang us from trees and expect our families to cut down the rope.

We went to bed last night angry, and we woke up today in rage. Anger, mixed with pain, underscored with agony. And the last thing we have the time, inclination or energy to do is make you feel better. Concern for your tears is no longer on our agenda.

The atonement that you seek can only be found by looking in the mirror.

DEAR WHITE WOMEN, IT'S NOT ABOUT YOU.

In 'today's "woke" climate, everyone is fighting to show the world that they are socially aware. Gone are the convenient days of saying, "My best friend is Black." Now, White women must use buzzwords like intersectionality, diversity, and inclusion to show Black women and Women of Color that they are down for the cause, they understand our oppression, and they stand with us in the fight.

Many celebrities understand in this socially connected and aware world that merely being a movie star is no longer enough. Nowadays, society requires that celebrities stand up and speak out, using their influence, prestige, and wealth to impact injustice.

Over the past weekend, many celebrities did speak up as this nation was once again reminded just how deep the roots of racism and hate go when mass shootings took place hours apart in El Paso, Texas, and Dayton, Ohio. Dozens of innocent people were murdered and many others injured as 2 White men hunted them like prey. In El Paso, the 21-year-old murderer, Patrick Crusius, wrote a manifesto filled with hate and racism towards immigrants that often echoed the sentiments spoken by Donald Trump. And the nation pretended to be surprised by the fact that words matter and the President of the United States is a racist that stokes the fires of hate through his racist rhetoric. Black people and People of Color have said this repeatedly only this time there has been just enough bloodshed that the nation is paying attention. How much more blood needs to spill before this nation comes to grips with the fact that indeed they voted for and put a racist into the highest office in the land?

This new level of surprise is impressive when the reality is what the reality is. Donald Trump did not waltz into The Oval; many people helped place him there. Fifty-three percent of White women that voted, voted for Donald Trump, helping to secure his position of power. And now here we are today as this nation is screaming, and White women are surprised. Let's be clear, Donald Trump never hid who he was as a person, and White women were okay with that. However, the problem with being okay with "a little bit of racism," is that there are no levels of racism. Being a "little racist" is like being a little pregnant. You either are, or you are not.

So now that this nation is realizing what Black people have tried to tell you everyone wants to step forward and make a statement to prove they are "woke." Perhaps that is what Rosanna Arquette thought when she took to Twitter to state, "'I'm sorry I was born White and privileged. It disgusts me. And I feel so much shame."

Really, Rosanna? Being born White and privileged disgusts you? You feel so much shame? Really?

And you think that tweet does what? Endear Black women to you? Make us say, "Awwwww?" Should we all break out our tissues and console you? Should we offer you a cookie? Should we say, "Look how "woke," Rosanna is?"

What did Rosanna think she was going to accomplish with that tweet?

White Women if you want to help Black women do not be like Rosanna. Rosanna comment is self-serving, which is often what White Feminism is all about. It seeks not to put the attention on Black women and Women of Color but always aims to put the focus on White women. Rosanna's tweet makes her feel better in the moment, and people can tell her, "Oh Rosanna we love you and appreciate you, and you are doing your best. Here, why don't try one of these chocolate chip I-am-not-a-racist-cookies I made." White Feminism always needs a participation trophy.

WAKE UP ROSANNA AND WHITE WOMEN LIKE ROSANNA; IT IS NOT ABOUT YOU!!!!

No one on this earth faults Rosanna or ANY White person for being White, having privilege and wealth. NO ONE! But she KNOWS that, but somehow she had to find a way to make it about her.

Take yourself OUT OF THE CENTER WHITE WOMEN! It is okay to stand with Black people, to understand injustice and NOT MAKE IT ABOUT YOU! It isn't about your "sadness" because you are White and privileged. What Black women have always asked is how are you using your privilege to help others that are not privileged? How are you using your influence to impact others? How are you using your wealth to support people that fight for justice? How are you using your voice to advocate on behalf of women who will NEVER be in the rooms you are in, who will NEVER be invited to the table? How are you doing that?

Making some self-serving, woe is me for being White, tweet that is dripping in White Feminism does absolutely nothing! It does nothing because you get to go back to your home and your wealth and your privilege while Black women and

Women of Color are still fighting for justice all while burying our loved ones that were taken far too soon through acts of hate fueled by racism. But sure, let us pause in our pain and our anguish to wipe away your tears because you are sad that you are White and privileged.

DEAR WHITE PEOPLE, BEFORE YOU POST DR. KING QUOTES TO MAKE YOURSELF FEEL GOOD...

Each January marks the date that many in the nation will observe Dr. Martin Luther King Jr. and the dedication and sacrifices he made as a civil rights activist. I will not use this article to detail the important and honorable aspects of Dr. King's life as countless details are readily available in books, online articles, magazines, videos, documentaries, and museums. I recall as a young girl being taught about Martin Luther King Jr. marching, preaching, and pushing a nation towards freedom. Dr. King is often cast as docile, peaceful and in contrast to a what some considered a more radical activist during his time, Malcolm X.

White America has created a Martin Luther King Jr. that it can stomach. White America has whitewashed Martin Luther King Jr. just enough that when it comes time to speak about race relations, Dr. King's words are the first that they turn to, just add I Have A Dream Speech and stir. White America is quick to quote Dr. King when they are attempting to 'put Black America in its place' when Black America is demanding justice. White America has watered down the message of Dr. King so severely that one minute according to Trump, Africa is a shithole and the next minute Trump can quote lines from Dr. King's I Have A Dream Speech without batting an eye.

So, before you rush to Google on Monday to search for a quote that you can tweet by Dr. King, I would ask that you look at the totality of his life and message and hold it up to the way you live your life. Do not merely quote words that make you feel good and do not challenge your thinking and actions. Do not tweet quotes that are nothing more than a Twitter performance when in actuality you have done nothing to support the causes that impact Black America. Do not use Dr. King's quotes as a way to "check" Black America. Do not ask Black America, "What would Martin Luther King Jr. do?" when it was White America that killed him.

When you want to tell Black America, there is a better way of protesting be reminded that Dr. King said: "We know through painful experience that freedom is never voluntarily given by the oppressor; it must be demanded by the oppressed. Frankly, I have yet to engage in a direct action campaign that was "well timed" in the view of those who have not suffered unduly from the disease of segregation. For years now I have heard the word "Wait!" It rings in the ear of every Negro with piercing familiarity. This "Wait" has almost always meant "Never." We must come to see, with one of our distinguished jurists, that "justice too long delayed is justice denied."

When you tell Black America, "Well it's the law," be reminded that Dr. King said, "We should never forget that everything Adolf Hitler did in Germany was legal."

When you ask us why we are fighting for justice be reminded that Dr. King said, "Oppressed people cannot remain oppressed forever. The yearning for freedom eventually manifests itself."

When you are quick to speak about Dr. King's dream be reminded that Dr. King also said, "About two years ago now, I stood with many of you who stood there in person and all of you who were there in spirit before the Lincoln Memorial in Washington. As I came to the end of my speech there, I tried to tell the nation about a dream I had. I must confess to you this morning that since that sweltering August afternoon in 1963, my dream has often turned into a nightmare. I've seen my dream shattered as I've walked the streets of Chicago and see Negroes, young men, and women, with a sense of utter hopelessness because they can't find any jobs. I've seen my dream shattered as I've been through Appalachia, and I've seen my white brothers along with Negroes living in poverty. And I'm concerned about white poverty as much as I'm concerned about Negro poverty."

When you condemn Black men and women, who have fought for this country and still can't find peace and justice in America, remember that Dr. King said, "So we have been repeatedly faced with the cruel irony of watching Negro and white boys on TV screens as they kill and die together for a nation that has been unable to seat them together in the same schools. So we watch them in brutal solidarity burning the huts of a poor village, but we realize that they would never live on the same block in Detroit. I could not be silent in the face of such cruel manipulation of the poor."

When you question as to why we are STILL fighting for just remember Dr. King said these words over 55 years ago and not much has changed, "But one hundred years later, the Negro still is not free. One hundred years later, the life of the Negro is still sadly crippled by the manacles of segregation and the chains of discrimination. One hundred years later, the Negro lives on a lonely island of poverty in the midst of a vast ocean of material prosperity. One hundred years later, the Negro is still languishing in the corners of American society and finds himself an exile in his own land. So we have come here today to dramatize a shameful condition."

When you want us to sit down and remain silent and just be content remember that Dr. King said, "It would be fatal for the nation to overlook the urgency of the moment. This sweltering summer of the Negro's legitimate discontent will not pass until there is an invigorating autumn of freedom and equality. Nineteen sixty-three is not an end, but a beginning. Those who hope that the Negro needed to blow off steam and will now be content will have a rude awakening if the nation returns to business as usual. There will be neither rest nor tranquility in America until the Negro is granted his citizenship rights. The whirlwinds of revolt will continue to shake the foundations of our nation until the bright day of justice emerges."

When you ask Black people why we protest when our brothers and sister are murdered by the police, remember that Dr. King said, "A man dies when he refuses to stand up for that which is right. A man dies when he refuses to stand up for justice. A man dies when he refuses to take a stand for that which is true. So we're going to stand up amid horses. We're going to stand up right here in Alabama, amid the billy-clubs. We're going to stand up right here in Alabama amid police dogs, if they have them. We're going to stand up amid tear gas! We're going to stand up amid anything they can muster up, letting the world know that we are determined to be free!"

When you question why Colin Kaepernick is kneeling and say that you don't disagree with him but just wish the protests were done a different way, when you ask me to "tone down" my blog so I don't offend White people, remember Dr. King said, "First, I must confess that over the past few years I have been gravely disappointed with the white moderate. I have almost reached the regrettable conclusion that the Negro's great stumbling block in his stride toward freedom is not the White Citizen's Counciler or the Ku Klux Klanner, but the white moderate, who is more devoted to "order" than to justice; who prefers a negative peace which is the absence of tension to a positive peace which is the presence of justice; who constantly says: "I agree with you in the goal you seek, but I cannot agree with your methods of direct action"; who paternalistically believes he can set the timetable for another man's freedom; who lives by a mythical concept of time and who constantly advises the Negro to wait for a "more convenient season." Shallow understanding from people of good will is more frustrating than absolute misunderstanding from people of ill will. Lukewarm acceptance is much more bewildering than outright rejection."

When you refuse to use your voice and privilege to challenge racism, when your first response to injustice is "not me" or "not all" remember Dr. King said, "In the end, we will remember not the words of our enemies but the silence of our friends."

I challenge you on Martin Luther King Day and **every day** to move beyond as Dr. King's daughter, Bernice King, stated, "#MLK Lite." What are you doing to become the dream that Martin spoke about? How are you using your voice to spread a message of peace, love and compassion? How are you using your wisdom to educate others about racism and injustice? How are you using your privilege and power to stand up for others? Dr. Martin Luther King Jr. has left his legacy. What will you do to leave yours?

BECKY, UGG BOOTS AND PUSSY CAT HATS

While many are celebrating the Women's March On Washington that happened January 21 2017, I sat on my couch staring at the TV feeling more irritated than inspired. I watched crowds of thousands, overjoyed that finally the message of racism, sexism, homophobia, and any other ism was finally being spread to the masses. The rally cry of, "Our rights are under attack", was the theme of the day. I wondered as I turned off the TV, 'where had these women been'? And then this picture came across my social media feed and it summed up everything that I was feeling. A Black woman stood with a sign that shouted the truth, that indeed the majority of White women voted for Trump, as three White women stood behind her, on their phones, taking selfies, as if they were asleep at the wheel. There it was. Everything that I was feeling. A Black woman hard at work to fight injustice and the White women asleep at the wheel or listening to someone give a speech that indeed we had shouted a million times before yet no one heard us.

I was not inspired. I was frustrated. I wanted to scream, WHERE WERE YOU?!

Where were you when we shouted about Sandra Bland dying on a jailhouse floor? Where were you when we screamed for your husbands to stop fucking us and raping our daughters?

Where were you when Anita Hill was vilified for speaking up against sexual harassment? Where were you when former officer and convicted rapist, Daniel Holtzclaw, raped Black women?

Where were you when we buried our sons and daughters?

Where were you when Dajerria Becton had a knee on her back and was assaulted by an officer? Where were you when a young Black girl was thrown across a classroom? Where were you when Alesia Thomas uttered, "I Can't Breathe", after getting kicked in the throat and groin in the back of a patrol car in 2012, before it became a slogan? Where were you when we marched for Mike Brown and Trayvon Martin? Where were you when we demanded that Black women MATTERED in this fight against police brutality?

Where were you when this nation sterilized Black, Native American and Puerto Rican women without their consent? Where were you when Michelle Obama was called an ape, evil, ugly?

Where were you then?

Similar to the photo of Angela Peoples holding a sing that said, "Don't Forget White Women Voted

For Trump," as she stood in front of three White women taking selfies, you were on your proverbial phone. Resting in your comfort. Sleeping on your bed of privilege. Oblivious to our cries. Turned a deaf ear to our shouts. Until you woke up Wednesday, November 9, 2016 and Trump and his impending policies had stepped on your rose-colored glasses. Until it was your freedoms that were threatened. Until they were coming for your birth control. Until your choice of whether to have a child was in jeopardy. Until it suddenly became inconvenient to just be Becky with the good hair. Until then you were content. You were complacent. It was easy to just appropriate a culture with no connection or concern for the people. It is easy to play the part of Miley Cyrus twerking in your skinny jeans with no regard of the Mapouka dance done in the Ivory Coast of the Dabon. A dance done by our ancestors at religious ceremonies that were culturally respected because they specifically believed that the dance brings them into an encounter with God. It is safe to wear "boxer braids" because Kim Kardashian did with no concern about the origin and the symbolism of a people that were skilled in agriculture. A hair style traced back to warriors, queens and kings. It was easy to dance along to Beyoncé's Formation with no clue or desire to know the underlying message she was trying to get across. And it is easy to march alongside people struggling, staring at your cellphones, in

UGG Boots, designer jackets and knitted pink pussy cat hats, taking selfies and curating hashtags for the memories. So thanks for the memories.

Enjoy your Woodstock euphoria as you go home. Back to your lives. Your sanctuary.

And for others the saga and struggle continue. We are here, as we have always been, and if indeed you are about that life, we welcome you for the long haul.

Look! It's a Bird, It's A Plane, It's Becky To the Rescue. My Thoughts On A Day Without Women

Have you ever experienced something and it just seemed off? You couldn't quite put your finger on it but something in your gut said, "This isn't right. There is something just slightly off about this." Perhaps like when you view those Spot The Difference pictures and the pictures look so incredibly similar yet under close, eagle-eyed scrutiny you notice slight differences.

That is how I felt about the Day Without Women. I wanted to stand behind it, wanted to support it, wanted to believe that maybe this time, they got it, they understood, they learned from the Women's March. Surely Becky, UGG Boots and Pussy Cat Hats was not going to be replicated but something in my gut said this is not right.

I felt like Smokey in Friday, "You ain't never got two things that go together...cereal, no milk; Kool-Aid, no sugar; ham, no burger...damn!!" I felt like they had protests for women, yet limited, if any, marginalized women. Protests, yet no acknowledging 53% of White women voted for Trump. Protests, not acknowledging their role in the history of oppression of many women. Protests, not understanding that the very fabric of the protest highlighted privilege. A privilege to take a day off work. A privilege that many Black Women and Women of Color do not possess.

Every woman does not have the privilege just to take off work. And while I know the outline allowed for this and said women on this day should wear red, I thought of women in uniforms. I thought of women that are stay at home mothers. How do they take a day off? Should they tell their children, "I am sorry, I am off today." I thought of single mothers getting up before the sun rises to head to a job that will not allow them a day to protest. I thought of many Women of Color working diligently to make ends meet all across this world.

Then I thought of women like my former teacher Ms. Brown, a Black woman, who told me my voice commanded attention even in 3rd grade. I thought of her and how her attention and nourishing of my writing and speaking, helped empower me to be who I am today. I thought of doctors, judges, bus drivers, waitresses, teachers, lawyers, professors, nurses that would be there March 8 and March 9 and March 10 and beyond because their passion and purpose are not about a National Women's Day Off. It is not about hashtags and selfies. It is about standing in the gap. It is about being a presence in a space when women need to be in those spaces. And they know standing in those spaces is an act of justice. We don't just walk off the job. We complete the job. We lay the foundation for other women to come behind us.

A Day Without Women is not symbolic of justice. It is not symbolic of equality. A Day Without Women is a day of hell. Without the backbone of this nation. A day without women is a day when the world has gone silent. And now more than ever is when we need women to shout!

Please, stop this! If you want to IMPACT this world use your power to disrupt policy that seeks to abuse the least of those. Use your privilege to stand up for someone that doesn't have the same privileges as you. Use your position to allow access for all women. Use your resources to fund a movement.

Right here in this nation reproductive rights are being taken away. Right here in this nation 10 and 11 years old girls are being trafficked. Right here in this nation Women of Color are dying from preventable diseases due to lack of health care. Right here Black women are murdered by the police and no one bats an eye. Right here they are passing laws to re-segregate schools. Right here they are passing legislation to criminalize protesting. Right here 6 Black transgender women and 1 Indigenous transgender woman have been murdered this year. Right here! Right at your very doorstep lies your protest. You don't have to look far to save the world. You don't need a spotlight to do the right thing. There are no hashtags needed when it comes to fighting for justice. As a matter of fact, we don't need you to save the world. Just save your own little corner. Start there. Forget the catchy slogans and cute knitted hats, and fancy curated posters and designer protest bumper stickers. Look around your community, your city, your state. There is where you will find a movement that needs you! Your voice! Your power! Your abilities!

Until then something will always seem off to me about these national "protests". Something will always seem "missing" like when you sit down at a meal and something just tastes off. Like it needs a little more pepper. A little more "seasoning". That is how I feel about these national "protests". They need some flavor. Until then everything will continue to taste bland and leave people wanting more.

WHITE WOMEN ARE ALWAYS ALLOWED TO BE THE VICTIM

As the not guilty verdict hit social media feeds around the world, it left many Black people just nodding their heads, as Officer Betty Shelby was able to exit an Oklahoma courtroom a free woman. Officer Shelby would not be held accountable for fatally wounding African American motorist Terence Crutcher. Justice once again found a way to laugh in the face of African Americans. If Lady Justice is blind, she sure has 20/20 vision when it comes to allowing White officers to walk free after they murder Black civilians. While I would like to say that I am shocked and stunned by the verdict, I am not. Betty Shelby joins a long a line of White women in America who are afforded the permission to be the victim especially when it comes to encounters with African American men.

When Shelby broke her silence about the fatal encounter with Crutcher, she made sure to note that he was "about 6 feet tall and 240 pounds." While Shelby contends that Crutcher's race and body size did not influence her decision to murder him in the middle of the street, it echoes an officer's comments made from the helicopter that was recording the encounter, that Crutcher looks like a "bad dude." I am curious, if Crutcher had no weapons and admittedly Shelby said that Crutcher was not acting aggressively, what would make a man all the way in a helicopter ascertain that Crutcher looked like a "bad dude"?

It is always funny to me how when a Black man is involved in a situation with the police their height, and weight always becomes a determining factor when deciding if they should live or die. We saw this countless times over when Mike Brown was made to appear as the Incredible Hulk and Tamir Rice, a 12-year-old boy who was shot and killed by an officer on a playground in less than 2 minutes. The news media focused on the height, and weight of Tamir instead of an emphasis on the fact that this was a 12-year-old child was murdered by the police.

This is often how the media generates the story when it comes to race relations. Black men are always painted as large, dark, menacing, evil and overpowering figures. And White women are painted as the innocent, demure, vulnerable victims that need to be coddled and protected especially from Black men that seek to harm them usually in a sexually violent manner. This is a narrative that has been generated since slavery. However, we know that indeed it was White slaveowners and their wives that abused, humiliated, whipped, raped and murdered Black men and women. White America has created, perpetuated and sold this myth to the world that it is not them that have committed some of the most if not THE most heinous crimes against humanity, but it is Black people, especially Black men that seek to harm White women.

The media continues to bolster this narrative with the damsel in distress theme. It is always a White woman that must be rescued from impending harm. From books to movies to fairytales White women are always portrayed as the innocent, demure, feminine and sexual being that must be rescued from the stereotype of the wild, savage and brutal Black man. Little girls are born and raised with images of Disney Princesses like Snow White and Cinderella, that must be rescued by their knight in shining armor. Black women are never portrayed in a way that would allow them humanity and vulnerability. Even when Disney did finally make a movie, The Princess, and the Frog, with a Black female lead character, it was not the prince that saved Tiana; it was Tiana that saved the prince. Black women are never allowed to be seen as vulnerable and in need of being rescued. Black women are never allowed to be the victim.

Similar to the narrative White America has sold about the savage and brute Black men, White America has developed and perpetuated the narrative that Black women are always the strong, wide-hipped, asexual, sassy, loud talking, side kick that is always there to provide a shoulder to cry on for White women with a finger snap, neck roll and an ounce of humor. This myth is bolstered in Hollywood with the mammy character in Gone With the Wind, Hattie McDaniel, the Black assistant coming to save the day played by Jennifer Hudson in Sex And The City, and Regina Long's character in Miss Congeniality. Black women are never portrayed as needing compassion and understanding.

This manifest beyond the big screen to real life when White women are often glorified and made into heroes for committing violent acts. Instead of portraying White women as violent murderers the media will often portray them as meek, innocent and as a woman that was pushed beyond her control. Even when White women commit some of the most heinous crimes, they are portrayed as the victim, and we are not called to vilify them but to understand them and sympathize with them. From murderers Jodi Arias, Laurie Bambenek, and Betty Broderick to child molesters, Mary Kay Letourneau, Deborah LaVave and Pamela Rogers Turner, the world attempts to make White women that commit crimes heroes and their actions excusable and acceptable. Betty Shelby stands in line with a list of White women that have circumvented justice.

White America continues to perpetuate the strong Black women myth because it absolves them of any guilt for how they treat Black women. Indeed, Black women are strong because we have always had to be strong. Society never gave us the luxury of breaking down. Society never gave us the luxury of taking a day off. Society never gave us the luxury to mourn. Society never gave us the luxury to be vulnerable. And because it never did, it does not have to see us that way, and that is why we can be abused, overlooked, overworked, raped, and beaten, and we are just supposed to be able to take it with a sister girl smile and a high five.

I understand that Black women make this look easy but we are not leprechauns or your magical Negro. Despite us declaring that Black women possess Black Girl Magic, there is nothing magical about this. What you don't acknowledge is Black mothers burying their sons and daughters, Black women putting up with sexual harassment at work because they have to put food on the table, Black women that are raped by an officer and too afraid to speak out because who would believe them anyway? What you don't see is a Black girl with an officer's knee in her back coming from a day at the swimming pool, or a Black girl thrown across a classroom like a ragdoll by a White officer because she is not moving as quickly as he would like. What you don't recognize is that Black women hurt and bruise and bleed. There is nothing race specific about pain and hurt and depression. There is nothing race specific about vulnerability. There nothing race specific about being the victim. For centuries Black women have had to go to rest in a bed of despair, crying tears into our pillows of heartache and no one ever stops to recognize that we hurt too. Sometimes we need to be rescued. There are days that we need to be seen as meek and soft and gentle and kind because that is who we are. Being a Black woman does not absolve us from heartache and pain and it certainly never seems to absolve us from the long arm of the law.

Am I surprised Betty Shelby walked out of a courthouse free to go home to her family while Terence Crutcher's family visits him at a graveyard? Not in the least bit. Betty always had two things working in her favor. She is an officer, and she is a White woman. America believes that officers are always innocent and White women are always the victim. Betty was never going to be convicted because she had everything working in her favor. It's the American Way.

THE PROBLEM IS NOT THE KKK; IT IS WELL-MEANING WHITE PEOPLE

In the Letter from Birmingham Jail, Martin Luther King Jr. wrote, "First, I must confess that over the past few years I have been gravely disappointed with the white moderate. I have almost reached the regrettable conclusion that the Negro's great stumbling block in his stride toward freedom is not the White Citizen's Counciler or the Ku Klux Klanner, but the white moderate, who is more devoted to "order" than to justice; who prefers a negative peace which is the absence of tension to a positive peace which is the presence of justice; who constantly says: "I agree with you in the goal you seek, but I cannot agree with your methods of direct action"; who paternalistically believes he can set the timetable for another man's freedom; who lives by a mythical concept of time and who constantly advises the Negro to wait for a "more convenient season." Shallow understanding from people of good will is more frustrating than absolute misunderstanding from people of ill will. Lukewarm acceptance is much more bewildering than outright rejection."

Similarly, to Dr. King's thinking, while the KKK and other racist groups exist, I am not overly concerned with the Richard Spencer's of the world. In fact, if I may be honest, on some level I can respect Richard Spencer for saying exactly who he is and exactly what he stands for. There is no in between or gray areas with Spencer. He wears his beliefs about race on his sleeve. Please do not misunderstand, I do not agree with any of the racist rhetoric that spills from his mouth, and I certainly do not condone any of his tactics or the tactics of others that seek to harm and disenfranchise people due to their race. However, when it comes to racism, I like racists to be the same way I like my Kentucky bourbon, straight with no chaser.

It is not the Richard Spencer's of the world that are causing me any problems. It is well-meaning White people that believe they could never be racist, that think because they are married to a Black man or woman or have Black friends they are not like "them." It was well-meaning White people that owned slaves. It was well-meaning White people that remained silent as Black people were lynched. It is well-meaning White people that read my blog and send me messages that say, "I should speak about love and not hate." It is the well-meaning White people that say, "I understand slavery but y'all should get over it." It is the well-meaning White people that believe they are not racist because they do community work in Black neighborhoods, donate to the NAACP and know all the dance moves to Single Ladies. It is well-meaning White people that believe there is nothing wrong with Confederate statues, trying to convince Black people that this issue of removing them is truly about history. It is well-meaning White people that will cheer for their NFL team powered by Black men but refuse to understand why Colin Kaepernick is kneeling. It is well-meaning White people that chose race over humanity when they voted Donald Trump into the highest office in the land. It is well-meaning White people that refuse to believe the statistics about the election results because they are too embarrassed to look in the mirror. It is well-meaning White people that can look at a video of a police officer saying, "We only kill Black people," and try to convince Black people that have suffered under the weight of police brutality that he was "only making a joke." For the mere fact, well-meaning White people are trying to convince Black people that this officer was making a joke, means they never understood our fight against police brutality. If so, they would understand that there is no humor when it comes to the death of Black men and women at the hands of the police.

When it comes to racism, well-meaning White people are a part of the problem.

While I applaud well-meaning White people for marching, tweeting, sharing an article, attending anti-racism meetings, if we are going to combat racism, it must be a little bit more personal to you. There is no benefit of continuing to preach to the choir. The choir is not your audience or your amen corner. It is time for you to decide which side you are on, friend. And should you choose the side of righteousness, compassion, liberation, and humanity, it will mean having some uncomfortable conversations, some that must start at your dining room table. There are conversations well-meaning White people need to have with their husbands, wives, children, girlfriends or boyfriends. There are neighbors that you will need to address. There are jokes that cannot be tolerated in the coffee break room. There are words you cannot tolerate in your presence or out of your presence. There is Facebook friends and family that you need to educate about racism. There are policies that you must speak out against. There are sacrifices you will have to make for the good of the many. There are Black people fighting that you must stand with on the front lines. Liberation will not be won in the shadows. Liberation demands the spotlight. It is time out for hidden allies. If you stand with us, stand with us in word and deed.

Well-meaning White people have stood by long enough. Well-meaning White people have remained silent long enough. Well-meaning White people have wavered in the winds of justice long enough. In the words of Florence Reece, "Which side are you on, friend?" The line has been drawn in the sand. And for those well-meaning evangelicals that believe they are doing their

Christian duty, like Paula White, let me quote Revelation, "I know your deeds, that you are neither cold nor hot. I wish you were either one or the other! So, because you are lukewarm—neither hot nor cold—I am about to spit you out of my mouth."

Make a choice. And if not, at the very least, stop pretending.

WERE WE NOT ENOUGH?

In recent weeks with the tragic and unfortunate murder of Heather Heyer, it seems the world has turned its eye to the United States of America, wagging its finger in shame. The blatant acts of racism that ascended upon Charlottesville, Virginia have been rebuked by actors, comedians, senators, congressmen, congresswomen, reporters, CEOs, restaurant owners, even some law enforcement, and everyday people in the world. The funeral of Heather Heyer was attended by hundreds and the events of that tragic day many have said impacted the very course of the presidency. Heather's last Facebook quote, "If you are not outraged, you are not paying attention," has been shared countless times on social media.

Indeed, either America was not paying attention or simply did not care because the people screaming for justice were Black. The recent events that have shaken this nation for many Black people and I are not new.

Let me be clear before I go any further; this is not an indictment on Heather, the life she led and the life she sacrificed for justice. Heather did Heather's part. And Heather lived her life in a way according to her mother, that was always about standing up for others. I believe that

Heather, with her last quote, would share my sentiments in this blog.

Recently in Kentucky, residents were asked to fill out a form about statues that "can be interpreted to be honoring bigotry, racism, and slavery." I posted the link on my social media accounts and encouraged people to complete the form, but as I was filling it out, I thought, "Why must I complete a form to speak to my humanity? Why do I need to complete a form for people to review it to decide if a statue erected in honor of someone that stood for racism should be taken down? Why is my humanity regulated to an online form?"

In the wake of this recent uprising for justice, I cannot help but ask as a Black woman, mother, poet, and activist, were we, as Black people, not enough?

When we took to the streets, we were labeled as thugs and degenerates, but now people taking to the streets are labeled the resistance, were we not enough?
When we stood in the streets screaming for justice after the murder of Mike Brown, were we not enough?
When we took over the streets of Ferguson, Missouri fighting for justice, were we not enough?
When we watched in horror as Philando Castile bled out on Facebook Live, were we not enough?
When we screamed, "Wrong!" as we watched Eric

Garner choked by an NYPD officer, were we not enough?
When we screamed for justice after Trayvon Martin was killed simply walking home after buying Skittles and tea, were we not enough? When we yelled for justice after Sandra Bland was found dead on a jailhouse floor, WERE WE NOT ENOUGH?
When we openly mourned after watching Rodney King beaten on a grainy video, were we not enough?

When we wept watching 7-year-old Aiyana Stanley-Jones (killed by the police) grandmother testify in open court, were we not enough?

When we watched in horror as a young Black girl was thrown across her class room by an officer, were we not enough?

When we stood in disbelief as no one was found guilty after the death of Rekia Boyd, were we not enough?

When we expressed outraged that countless police officers were found not guilty after senseless killings, were we not enough? When we stood up against monuments erected to uphold the mentality of a slave nation, were we not enough?

When we fought to bring down monuments built in honor of those that supported the institution of slavery, and no one heard us, were we not enough?

When we took to Twitter with the #NoConfederate hashtag and David Benioff, Dan Weiss and HBO turned a blind eye to our concerns, yet now the world sees pretending slavery never ended is not wise, were we not enough?

When we watched the world spit in the face of Black America, were we not enough?

When we buried our Black sons and daughters too soon, were we not enough?

When we told you that you should be outraged, were we not enough?

It seems Black pain, suffering and injustice can only be understood by this world if it is viewed and encapsulated through the eyes of a White world.

I stand puzzled why so many White people are now surprised that America is not ice-cold lemonade and apple pie? Have Black people not been screaming this truth?

What did you think we meant when we told you Trump upheld a racist agenda? What do you think we meant when we told you Trump's slogan, Make America Great Again, really meant, Make America White Again? What did you think we meant when we said electing Barack Obama into office did not mean we entered a post-racial America? What do you think we meant when we said our reproductive rights were being stripped away daily? What did you think we meant when we told you that your healthcare would be impacted? What did you think we meant when we were protesting police brutality? What did you think we meant when we were on Twitter for weeks practically begging David Benioff, Dan Weiss and HBO not to promote a show about slavery never ending? What did you think we meant when we told you voting for Trump was a vote for racism and hatred? What do you think we meant when we were yelling for righteousness?

What I believe is that you thought it would never affect you. I believe you thought those are just some Black people making noise that you didn't want to hear. I believe you thought this hate, racism, and intolerance would never step on your front porch. But now you know, chickens always come home to roost. As Martin Luther King Jr, said, "We are caught in an inescapable network of mutuality, tied in a single garment of destiny. Whatever affects one directly, affects all indirectly."

There is no getting around us. We are not going anywhere. What we speak today and what my people have spoken about for years, is cold, hard, reality. The plane is now on fire.

One day I pray this world can take the truth of what Black people say straight with no a chaser. It is my hope that one day this world will listen when Black people speak. It is my hope that our cries against injustice won't need to be autotuned, laced over a trap beat to catch the frequency of White America. It is my hope that the truth that Black people speak will be taken at face value. It is my hope that White people will not continue to profit by studying what Black people have already told White America was true. It is my hope that Black people's cries for justice will not need to be White-splained. It is my hope that the struggles of being a Black woman in this world doesn't need to be decorated in pink pussy cat hats before it is considered truth. It is my hope that a White person will not write an op-ed about racial inequities and it gets more views, publicity and credibility than a Black person that has said the very same thing for years. It is my hope that no blood, neither White or Black needs to be shed before White America realizes the error of its ways. It is my hope that one day, White America will hear, listen and act when Black America speaks, and it will not need the filter of a White person to react to Black truth.

ROSE, WHITE FEMINISM & INTERSECTIONALITY (OR SOME OTHER BUZZWORD THAT'S HOT THIS MONTH)

Rose...Rose...Rose...

Really, Rose? In your righteous fight against men that have sexually assaulted women in Hollywood, you went overboard by saying being called a woman is comparable to being called the N-word. To double down on your ignorance, instead of apologizing to every Black woman that you offended, you blame your ~~now deleted~~ comments on smoking weed.

And THIS is my problem with White feminism and just how self-serving it is.

You see, we were rooting for you, Rose.

But still, I watched your comments on Twitter and never said a word because as much as I reveled in you and other women bringing down a seemingly lifelong sexual predator, I remember that it is some of these very same White women that didn't have any problem putting a man that said, "Just grab em by the p*ssy", into the highest office in the land. It is some of these very same White women standing with you, that never say a word when a Woman of Color is a victim. I have been in this world long enough to know that in your quest to

bring awareness to your issue, you would say something against Black women.
And without fail, you were right on cue.

Feminism and Black women aren't that difficult to understand, but for some reason, it appears White feminists continue to make misstep after misstep when it comes to Women of Color and feminism.

I am going to explain this as plainly as I can from my narrative of being a Black woman and a woman that believes in the liberation of ALL women. Of course, this list is not exhaustive but these steps should serve as a good start to combat White Feminism.

1.This is Hannah. Hannah is a woman AND Hannah is also Black.

2.Being a woman and being Black are <u>not</u> two separate issues for Hannah.

3. Hannah fights for justice and believes in the liberation of ALL women!

4. Not just SOME women.

5. Because Feminism does NOT just include cisgender heterosexual, able-bodied, middle and upper class White women.

6.Feminism is NOT about silencing Women of Color.

7.Feminism is NOT about ignoring issues that affect Women of Color because you think they do not directly affect you.

8. Feminism is NOT about stealing the creativity and ingenuity of Women of Color and pawning it off as your own in order to capitalize on it.

9.Feminism is NOT about equating the issues White women face with being called a n*gger or other racial slurs.

10. Feminism is NOT about making excuses when you have said or done something that is problematic or offends Women of Color.

11. Feminism is NOT about valuing the legacy of White supremacy over the interests of all women.

12. Feminism is NOT about appropriating the struggles of Women of Color or exploiting a cause that is centered around Black people to champion your cause.

13. Feminism is NOT about restricting Women of Color from the table.

14. Feminism is NOT about allowing one woman of color at the table to perpetuate the illusion of inclusion.

15. Feminism means getting your hands dirty and it will not always feel comfortable or have a cute hashtag, hat or ribbon to go along with it.

16. Feminism means looking in the mirror and having some tough conversations with yourself, then your friends and family about the privilege White women have in this world.

17. Feminism means admitting that you have not stood up for Women of Color because you didn't care or you didn't have to because you didn't see our issues as your issues and then making a conscious decision to do better.

18. Feminism is admitting that as a White woman you have benefitted from some of the very systems that have harmed Black Women and Women of Color and you remained silent. You have been complicit either as as active or silent co-conspirator in some of the very systems and policies that have harmed Women of Color.

19. Feminism means remembering it is not all about you, taking your ego out of it and refraining from calling Women of Color hostile, abrasive, disruptive or intimidating when we challenge your silo style of feminism.

20. Feminism means holding the door open, passing the mic and using your privilege to advocate on behalf of Women of Color.

21. Feminism means LISTENING to Women of Color when we speak.

22.Feminism means challenging policies that negatively impact the lives of Black Women and Women of Color.

23. Feminism means inviting ALL women to the table to share their voices, influence and power and not as an afterthought.

24. Feminism means if it is an issue for Black Women and Women of Color it is an issue for ALL women!

Any questions?

Dear Alyssa, Please Stop With Your Performative Twitter Social Justice

In January 2017, my blog begin with a critique of the Women's March, a march that was heavily and primarily attended by White women in knitted pink pussycat hats as if we had forgotten that indeed 53% of White women that voted, voted for Donald Trump. As I watched the march on TV, I struggled to figure out why it was not resonating with me. I am a woman that believes in the liberation of ALL women, but something was amiss. And then the iconic picture of Angela Peoples holding a sign that read, "Don't Forget White Women Voted For Trump, as three White women stood behind her taking selfies, came across my newsfeed and immediately I knew that was why I felt the way that I did.

While I support protesting, and marching I felt many of the White women during the November 2016 election were like the three White women in the background of the picture nonchalantly on their phones, taking selfies in their Ugg boots as if the proverbial plane was not on fire. However, the plane is on fire and has been on fire, but White America treated Black people, particularly Black women as if we were the stewardess giving instructions as the flight takes off for what to do if the plane goes down. We were tuned out, and our shouts ignored as White America went on about its business.

We were just those protestors fighting against racism until it was Heather Heyer. We were only those people complaining about police brutality until it was Alex Wubbels a White nurse being wrongly arrested by a Utah police. We were just overreacting when we screamed about Freddie Gray being given a "rough ride" by the police which aided in his death, and then the President of the United States encouraged police to rough up suspects. We were just those lone dissenters screaming about healthcare until you realized Trump meant your healthcare would be taken away too. We were just standing with a Black woman named Anita Hill that testified about sexual harassment against a man that went on to become a Supreme Court Justice and then it all hell broke loose in Hollywood. We told you we did not live in a post-racial America after the election of President Barack Obama and then 74% of White men and 65% of White women that voted in the Alabama Senate election, voted for a racist alleged pedophile and the world realized we were not post-racial. It seems life would be much less complicated if White America would listen to Black people, particularly Black women when we speak. And not as an afterthought but a forethought.

I started this year on a high note, believing that something that I wrote would shake up the world. Yet here we are just three days from a new year and actress turned activist, Alyssa Milano makes a Twitter post that revealed to me that we have a very long way to go. Alyssa was thrust into the spotlight after she tweeted a phrase "Me Too" to bring awareness to people that have been victims of sexual harassment and assault. However, the "Me Too" movement was actually started by a Black woman named, Tarana Burke over a decade ago. Alyssa later acknowledged this fact however what was done was done and many credit Alyssa with sparking a movement.

Perhaps Alyssa was feeling particularly revolutionary when she took to Twitter early in the morning to post the poem by Langston Hughes, Let America Be America Again. In her posting of the poem, she highlights a stanza by Hughes forgetting the central focus of the poem that Hughes places in parentheses, America never was America to me, almost as if he wants to draw particular attention to that part of the poem.

It is as if the ENTIRE meaning of the poem flew just north of Alyssa's head.

Alyssa's convenient performative act of justice reminds me of when White people cherry-pick quotes by Martin Luther King Jr. or Muhammad Ali that help them sleep better at night. Do not forget that while Dr. King said, "I have been to the mountaintop" he has also said, "First, I must confess that over the past few years I have been gravely disappointed with the white moderate. I have almost reached the regrettable conclusion that the Negro's great stumbling block in his stride toward freedom is not the White Citizen's Counciler or the Ku Klux Klanner, but the white moderate, who is more devoted to "order" than to justice; who prefers a negative peace which is the absence of tension to a positive peace which is the presence of justice; who constantly says: "I agree with you in the goal you seek, but I cannot agree with your methods of direct action"; who paternalistically believes he can set the timetable for another man's freedom; who lives by a mythical concept of time and who constantly advises the Negro to wait for a "more convenient season." Shallow understanding from people of good will is more frustrating than absolute misunderstanding from people of ill will. Lukewarm acceptance is much more bewildering than outright rejection."

While people like Alyssa love to quote Muhammad Ali saying, "Service to others is the rent you pay for your room here on earth," do not forget that Ali also said, "I ain't draft dodging. I ain't burning no flag. I ain't running to Canada. I'm staying right here. You want to send me to jail? Fine, you go right ahead. I've been in jail for 400 years. I could be there for 4 or 5 more, but I ain't going no 10,000 miles to help murder and kill other poor people. If I want to die, I'll die right here, right now, fightin' you, if I want to die. You my enemy, not no Chinese, no Vietcong, no Japanese. You my opposer when I want freedom. You my opposer when I want justice. You my opposer when I want equality. Want me to go somewhere and fight for you? You won't even stand up for me right here in America, for my rights and my religious beliefs. You won't even stand up for my right here at home."

For Alyssa to conveniently highlight a part of Langston's poem that makes her feel good, that will get her some Twitter likes and then have the audacity to come back to Twitter to EXPLAIN what Langston meant in his poem, as if Black people are not the walking living personification of his words is an insult to every Black person on this earth.

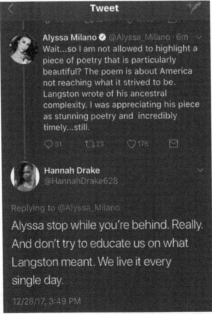

Let me educate you, Alyssa beyond your performative Twitter racial justice on what Langston meant. You have failed to highlight the most important part of his poem.Langston is writing about two things in extreme juxtaposition to draw a glaring difference in what America says it is and the reality of what America actually is for Black people.

Black people were brought to this land in chains, suffered some of the worst heinous, atrocious crimes against Black humanity, worked in fields from sun up to sun down expected to pick over 200 pounds of cotton a day, and suffered the whip of the lash if they didn't meet their quota. When you tweet, "Me Too" remember that it was enslaved Black women that were raped by White men and White people turned a blind eye. It was Black women that had to look into the eyes of their husbands while a slave master stole their humanity. It was Black women that had to birth children by their slave masters. Here in Kentucky where Langston's paternal great-grandfathers were slave owners, an enslaved Black woman named Lucy was lynched for murdering her slave owner and rapist. So no, Alyssa, America has never been America to me.

Black people have suffered under the weight of racism just to have civil rights. Black people were arrested, beaten, water hosed, had dogs turned loose on them just for the right to just be. A Black boy named Emmett Till was beaten and killed because he was falsely accused of talking to a White woman. This same White woman had the convenience of admitting that she lied years later.

How convenient it must be to take a stand for Black people you have harmed from the comfort of your home. Sound familiar, Alyssa? George Stinney, a 14-year-old Black boy, was sent to the electric chair for murders he did not commit. At just 90 pounds, George was so small that he had to sit on top of a Bible for the helmet of the electric chair to fit him for White America to make an example out of him. So no, Alyssa, America has never been America to me.

And here we are today with the murders of Trayvon Martin, Sandra Bland, Eric Garner and countless others. Today of all days for you to make your post, Black people are hurting as we stand in the gap for Erica Garner, the daughter of Eric Garner, a 27-year-old Black woman that fought for social justice after the murder of her father, that was declared brain dead after suffering a heart attack. Yet here you are with a misinterpreted poem from one of the most prolific writers that wrote for radical racial reform. Here we are in 2017 where the weight of racism continues to chip away at our lives daily. Here we are when a 12-year-old boy named Tamir Rice is gunned down on a playground by the police in less than 2 minutes for playing with a toy gun. Here we are where an NFL player can be vilified and blackballed for taking a knee to bring awareness to police brutality. Here we are, Alyssa, where a Black man can be wrongly murdered by the police on camera and America tries to tell us why it is justified. Here we are, Alyssa, where a Black man in Mississippi can be beheaded in 2017. Here we are, Alyssa, where Black people are STILL fighting for the right to just exist in America. So no, Alyssa, America has never been America to me.

And you come online with your Twitter post as if the world is supposed to be impressed by your performative social justice and ignorance. I am hardly impressed. It is easy to overlook Langston's meaning of his poem when you do not have to live it daily. It is easy to make a Twitter post and sit back and pat yourself on the back as people like your post and feel as if you have done something for the advancement of race relations in America. In fact, you have done nothing but show me that we still have a long road to travel.

As Langston wrote,

Who said the free? Not me?
Surely not me? The millions on relief today?
The millions shot down when we strike?
The millions who have nothing for our pay?
For all the dreams we've dreamed
And all the songs we've sung
And all the hopes we've held
And all the flags we've hung,
The millions who have nothing for our pay—
Except the dream that's almost dead today.
O, let America be America again—
The land that never has been yet—

Since you enjoy quoting Black writers, Alyssa, let me quote one for you. In the words of James

Baldwin, "I love America more than any other country in this world, and, exactly for this reason, I insist on the right to criticize her perpetually." And daily I will criticize America for what it isn't for Black people and ALL People of Color longing and screaming for JUSTICE!

ALL IT TAKES IS FOR ONE WHITE WOMAN TO PASS THE MIC

In 1940, Hattie Mae McDaniel received an Oscar for her role as Mammy in Gone With The Wind. The Los Angeles Times praised McDaniel's work as "worthy of Academy supporting awards," and indeed McDaniel went on to win an Oscar for Best Supporting Actress.

Many people viewed this as a turning point for the Oscars. However, they fail to mention that McDaniel was not allowed to sit at the table with cast members, Vivien Leigh and Clark Gable but had to sit at a table near a far way wall because the Ambassador Hotel, where the ceremony was held, had a strict No Blacks policy. The film's director, David O. Selznick, called in a favor just to have McDaniel allowed into the building. Her final wish, to be buried in the Hollywood Cemetery was denied because "the cemetery practiced racial segregation and would not accept the remains of Black people for burial."On one hand Hollywood might appear progressive during that time in awarding McDaniel the highest award in their industry, on the other hand, her honor was still undergirded by racism. In fact, it would take over fifty years, for a Black woman, Whoopi Goldberg, to accept an award for Best Supporting Actress again.

April Reign started an #OscarsSoWhite movement in response to the lack of diversity at the Oscars, but it speaks even more to the scripts that are being greenlit in Hollywood. Women of Color cannot win awards for roles they are never allowed to have. Roles that are never written with a Women of Color in mind. Stories that are never told about Women of Color. And indeed, Women of Color have a myriad of stories. Stories that are bubbling up inside of them, waiting to be told.

However, those that control who tells the stories, share the stories that they desire. So seeing the cover of LA Times The Envelope, doesn't shock me because White women are the default when it comes to most things in this world. White women are held up and presented as the standard. So when the LA Times decided it was going to do a story on "A Shift In Focus: Actresses Call For A Change In The Way Stories Are Told" and placed all White women on the cover and only enlisted the voices and opinions of White women, to them this is acceptable. Because White is the standard, they cannot even see the irony of the title of the article in juxtaposition to the photo. How many People of Color are on the staff of the LA Times? How many People of Color have power and influence at the LA Times? How many People of Color, write the stories at the LA Times? How do you write a story about the hit movie Get Out that challenges people to listen to Black people more and then do a article about shifting focus that is only centered around White women?

One of the actresses, Jessica Chastain, said in the article, "I'm open with my opinions because I've only been in the industry for six years. I started pretty late — 2011 is when my first film came out. I'd already had the great fortune of growing up out of the industry. I don't know how to not speak out. "
Jessica has even posted about the "unseen women" issue on Twitter. If Jessica was ever going to speak out about unseen and unheard women, during this interview and cover shoot would have been a great time.

All it would take is for ONE of those women to stand up and say, "Because we are talking about telling a new story, we should have a more diverse selection of women to tell their story in this article." That is how you change the world. That is how you show intersectionality not just in word but also in deed. However, when everything around tells you that as a White woman you are the standard, it is difficult to notice when someone isn't being represented. It takes making a CONSCIOUS DECISION TO CARE ENOUGH TO EVEN NOTICE AND THEN TO ACT. How could someone like Annette Bening, a legend in Hollywood, shift the entire focus of the article, if she stood up and said, "There are people missing from this discussion." She has influence, USE IT. One of the BENEFITS of having power is to USE IT for those that do not have it to impact their lives.

Representation matters. Seeing yourself reflected to you, can alter the course of your life because you start to believe that what the world has told you was impossible is in fact, possible. As a Women of Color, I am always looking for someone that looks likes me in a space. For someone that I believe will represent me and issues that impact Black women. For someone that can tell my side of the story in a room that I may never have the power or influence to be in. And when it is not represented it is glaringly apparent. However, it is oblivious to people who more than likely never have to think about being "the other." For instance, when Princess Michael of Kent wore a blackamoor brooch to the queen's annual Christmas lunch at Buckingham Palace some considered the brooch racist. In her apology, she said, "She has worn it before, and it has never caused any controversy." Just to make that statement shows how the world makes White the standard. I am going to assume in her social circle she is around people that look and think like her so naturally, it would not be a source of controversy. When you have always been the standard, you see nothing wrong with wearing a brooch that many consider similar to blackface. She never has to think about it; it is just normal to her.

When it comes to how we tell stories, I challenge White people, particularly White women, to take themselves out of the center and then ask themselves:

1. Am I making myself the center of this story?
2. Who is telling the story?
3. Are there Women of Color that should be telling this story?
4. Who benefits from this story?
5. Whose voice isn't being heard in this story?
6. What agenda is centered in this story?
7. Who is or isn't being represented in this story?
8. Are White people the default in this story?
9. How are People of Color portrayed in this story?
10. Have I thought about "the other"?

Seeing the La Times The Envelope cover, I was reminded of Viola Davis's Oscar speech:
"Thank you to the Academy. You know, there's one place that all the people with the greatest potential are gathered. One place and that's the graveyard. People ask me all the time, what kind of stories do you want to tell, Viola? And I say, exhume those bodies. Exhume those stories. The stories of the people who dreamed big and never saw those dreams to fruition. People who fell in love and lost. I became an artist — and thank God I did — because we are the only profession that celebrates what it means to live a life."

I became a writer to tell the stories and perspectives of Black Women. I want to read about characters that look like me and speak like me, that understand my "slang" and do not chastise me for my differences. I want to read stories where I am the center, where issues that impact me are the focus. I want to see me all around me. As my friend Kiara said, "The world is so much more beautiful when you can see yourself in it." I became a writer to put those stories into the atmosphere and to use my words to challenge people to tell a new narrative. All people have a story, and they deserve the right to tell their story. Open up your eyes and be amazed at how much more rich, glorious and full this world can be if the voices of all people are heard.

BLACK WOMEN DO NOT EXIST TO SAVE YOU

In a narrow win, Doug Jones has won the Senate race in Alabama. And by narrow, I mean less than 50,000 votes. So, before any of us break our arm off to pat ourselves on the back, remind yourself that this was a race between a man that prosecuted the KKK for the murder of 4 Black girls in a bombing at 16th Street Baptist Church and a man that is accused of being a pedophile. And it was still a narrow win. Let that sink in. We are that far gone in America that people considered alleged pedophile Roy Moore a viable candidate for Senate. As the rest of the nation waited for the results, articles begin to pop up online about Black people saving the Alabama election. And many people jumped on this sentiment as if this was a compliment. Then the hashtag, #TrustBlackWomen, started to make the Twitter rounds.

Admittedly, I have said Trust Black Women a million times because as a Black woman, I believe we hold the solutions to so many problems in the world. However, over time the mood and meaning of this hashtag started to shift for me. Trust Black women is now becoming synonymous with allow Black women to do the work that White people do not want to do. Trust Black women is now becoming synonymous with allow Black women to do the work for little to no pay. Trust Black women is now becoming synonymous with allow Black women to generate creative work and allow White people to take the credit. Trust Black women is now becoming synonymous with allow Black women to clean up our mess. Let me be clear, Black people, particularly Black women, do not exist to save White America from itself. Black people, particularly Black women, were not placed on this earth to rescue White people from themselves. To save yourself, you must take a long hard look in the mirror and put in the work. Our existence, brilliance, creativity, strength, and ingenuity can never be validated by you posting a hashtag that means nothing when your actions do not support what you project online. Trust Black Women means nothing if your policies and institutions do not seek to elevate Black women and help combat issues that impact Black women. Liking a tweet and posting #TrustBlackWomen so that you can get likes means nothing if you go to the voting booth and vote for someone that said slavery was a time when America was great. Quite frankly I feel like many of you post things that highlight Black women not because you genuinely care about Black women but because it garners you a lot of attention and likes. Your extent of concern when it comes to Black women is how many people will retweet your post because it's cool to be "down" with Black women online. However, the numbers don't lie.

Black women have warned you time and time again. And still, you do not listen. We warned you about Trump. You didn't listen. We warned you about the Governor race in Virginia. Still, you didn't listen. We warned you about Roy Moore and once again, you didn't listen.

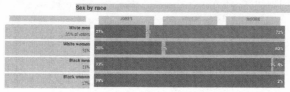

Exit poll results in Alabama.

At this point, I don't know what else you want. I don't want to receive one more email from a White woman that says, "Not me" or "Not All". I don't want to hear one more buzzword like intersectionality. I don't care how many Audre Lorde quotes you can recite.

Black women have done our share of the work.
Black women have carried the load until our backs have bent in agony.
Black women have smiled when all we wanted to do was cry.
Black women are tired.
Black women will no longer play wet nurse to White America.
At some point, you have to get off the breast and grow up.
We cannot nurse you through racial discord. We cannot hold your hand through fighting racism because both our hands are too busy fighting to save our lives and family's lives.

Throughout history, we have left breadcrumbs of our resistance. We have written the playbook on how to fight for liberation. From Oya to Vashti, to Harriet, to Fannie and beyond, we have drawn the blueprint.

It is time that you move from just hashtags to action. While I appreciate that you want to Trust Black Women, start learning how to trust yourself and do the work that will be required to shake a nation.

WHAT HAPPENS AFTER THE PINS, PINK PUSSY CAT HATS, AND WHITE ROSES?

Recently an article was published on PageSix entitled, These Men Forgot to Wear Their Times Up Lapel Pin to the SAG's as if they were finished with their support for the recent shaking up of Hollywood that demands women equality.

Is this really an issue? Because some male actors did not wear a Time's Up pin that means they do not or have stopped supporting women in our quest for equality?

Seriously? This is my problem when symbols start to overtake a movement. Please do not misunderstand, I understand that symbols matter. I will never forget the joy I felt in my heart to see Bree Newsome scramble up a flagpole to take down a racist symbol like the Confederate flag. I was filled with pride when I watched GreenSpace have Confederate statues removed from their parks in Memphis, Tennessee. And in Kentucky, where I live, I was happy to see that the Confederate statue that resided at the University of Louisville, was taken down. Hold up...relocated...so...

Then what?

What is happening in this world is bigger than pins, black couture gowns, pink pussycat hats or white roses.

What happens after the Time's Up pin?

What happens after the black couture gowns at the Golden Globes?

What happens after the Women's March?

What happens after you take the selfies of you at Women's March?

What happens after you have posted the catchy political sign to Instagram?

What happens after the white roses at the Grammy's?

What happens after you take off the pink pussycat hat?

And there you are, alone, staring at yourself in the mirror with no Starbucks, no catchy signs or would be campaign slogans, no rainbow sticker, no t-shirt. It is just you and your reflection. Your reflection along with a husband that tells you he hates niggers, a co-worker that makes offensive jokes about gay men, a Black woman working tirelessly in your department that you know is being paid 15% less for doing the same job as you, your neighbor that insists Trump is making America great again with his racism, family dinners with conversation that disparages immigrants...

Then what?
What happens then?

Because it is easy to get caught up in the symbols and the hype. It is easy to slide on your UGG boots and head out for a "day" of protesting. It is easy to knit a pink pussycat hat to cover your 200 dollar highlights. It is easy to grab a Sharpie and make a political sign with the hope that your sign will be picked up by the masses and garner you Twitter Revolutionary Credibility, but then what?

What happens after the rally high?

Can you stand in the fire?

Can you stand AFTER the rally?

Can you stand with a Black woman that is screaming for justice?

Can you pause and take yourself out of the center of a movement?

Can you understand that while you may have just entered this fight for justice MANY Women of Color have been yelling for centuries and our yells were met with silence?

Can you understand that our GOAL in life is not to SAVE YOU because we are trying to save ourselves?

Can you make yourself lesser so that a Person of Color can be greater?

Can you provide excess resources to a cause that fights against injustice?

Can you make your catchy signs the next time, because sadly, there will be a next time, a young Black or Brown person is killed by the police?

Can you resist the URGE to say, "Not Me?"

Can you admit that you have benefitted from systems that oppress People of Color?

Can you recognize that everything isn't about you?

Can you acknowledge that slavery impacted and altered the course of Black people in America?

Can you CARE when there is no celebrity endorsement?

Can you repost a tweet bringing awareness to injustice even if that means you will lose followers?

Can you understand that Black people do not have the time or inclination to be concerned with how our truth can and will make White people uncomfortable?

Can you admit that racism is at the very core of this nation, its policies, and laws?

Can you admit that EVEN YOU in your pink pussycat hat and pin, have been racist towards a Person of Color?

Can you march alongside a Mother of Color that has lost her child to police brutality?

Can you vote in favor of politicians that stand for the advancement of People of Color?

Can you advocate for immigrants that just want to come to this Native American land to make a better life for themselves?

Can you look your neighbor in the eye and tell them that Black people have the RIGHT to walk around your neighborhood freely?

Can you resist the urge to casually laugh at a joke told at the expense of minorities because your boss told the joke?

Can you admit that White Privilege is a thing?

Can you use your voice to advocate on behalf of those the world wishes would remain silent?
CAN YOU DO THAT?
Because truth be told, I don't give a fuck about your hat, your flower, your black couture gown or whatever new symbol will pop up in the next few months.
I GIVE A DAMN ABOUT JUSTICE!
AND JUSTICE DOESN'T RESIDE IN A PIN OR FLOWER.
IT RESIDES IN WHAT YOU DO AFTER THE RALLIES, CATCHY SIGNS, PINK PUSSYCAT HATS, AND TWITTER HASHTAGS.
JUSTICE STARTS AFTER THE IPHONE, ANDROID AND CAMERAS HAVE STOPPED CLICKING AND ROLLING!

IVANKA TRUMP'S OPRAH WINFREY TWEET IS A NAUSEATING DISPLAY OF WHITE FEMINISM

At the 75th Golden Globe Awards, as Oprah Winfrey came to the stage to accept the Cecil B. DeMille Award for lifetime achievement, we all wondered what Oprah would say to the world considering the recent #MeToo movement that has taken over Hollywood and a nation.

In true Oprah form, she made the moment not about her, but about the women that are fighting to endure both past and present. "What I know for sure," Oprah said, "is that speaking your truth is the most powerful tool we all have. And I'm especially proud and inspired by all the women who have felt strong enough and empowered enough to speak up and share their personal stories. Each of us in this room are celebrated because of the stories that we tell, and this year we became the story."

With her speech, many of us felt inspired, empowered, and invigorated. We felt that the world heard us. We felt that our voices had the force of the world behind them pushing us toward change.

The next night, Ivanka Trump piped up on Twitter to weigh in: "Just saw Oprah's empowering & inspiring speech at last night's Golden Globes.

Let's all come together, women & men, & say #TimesUp! United."

I paused in disbelief and shock. What planet does Ivanka live on?

In the world I live in, her father, President Donald Trump, has been accused of sexual misconduct by more than a dozen women. In the world that I live in, her father talks about moving on a woman like a bitch. In the world that I live in her father brags about kissing women without even waiting because, "When you are a star, they let you do it ... you can do anything." In the world that I live in, her father calls a grieving Gold Star widow a liar. In the world that I live in, her father mocks and calls a black congresswoman "wacky" when she stands up for a Gold Star widow. In the world that I live in, her father delights in tweeting about a woman's physical appearance in a negative way.

How dare Ivanka post #TimesUp while we are all watching the clock wondering when time is going to catch up with her father?

But perhaps I shouldn't have been surprised: White Feminism is clapping during Oprah's speech when she spoke of Recy Taylor, a young black woman who in 1944 was abducted while walking home from church in Alabama and raped by six white men, but turning out to vote for racist and alleged pedophile, Roy Moore, for Alabama senator, as more than 60 percent of white women did in the 2017 special election. White Feminism is

53 percent of the white women voting in the 2016 presidential election for a man who brags about grabbing women by the pussy. White Feminism is showing up to the Women's March in a pink hat without ever acknowledging that women of color have been doing this work for years.

White Feminism is performative justice that works to create the illusion of inclusion. White Feminism posts tweets about equality all while stepping on the backs of women of color. White Feminism knows all the buzzwords like diversity, inclusion, empowerment, and intersectionality. White Feminism wears the hip T-shirts with catchy feminist slogans like "Nasty Woman." White Feminism has a best friend who is a woman of color. White Feminism watches Insecure. White Feminism knows all the words to Beyonce's Lemonade album. White Feminism knows and tweets all the latest feminist hashtags. White Feminism quotes Audre Lorde.

But while doing all of that, White Feminism actually does nothing. White Feminism remains silent when it should be shouting. White Feminism doesn't understand that issues that impact women of color affect them too: When women of color are fighting for health care, we are not fighting for health care just for us. We are fighting so that you and your children can have health care too. When black women are protesting about our sons and daughters being disproportionally targeted and killed by the police, we are protesting on behalf of your children too. When women of color are fighting to be heard, it's because we know that our voices have the power to impact the world too. Yet White Feminism believes it has the authority to speak for all women instead of passing the mic. White Feminism exists in a bubble. White Feminism pretends it cares about the needs of all women when in fact it only seeks to serve itself.

That is precisely what Ivanka Trump did when she retweeted Oprah Winfrey's speech.

Oprah is a black woman who, unlike Donald Trump, is a self-made billionaire. A black woman born into poverty in Mississippi to a single mother. A black woman who was molested and became pregnant at 14 years old. A black woman whose child died in infancy. A black woman who is a billionaire and still must contend with racism. A black woman that has dedicated her life to advancing others. Oprah stood in that space on Sunday night and spoke truth to power. Oprah spoke truth in the face of white women like Ivanka who use their power and influence to do nothing. Ivanka's tweet is performative White Feminism that looks good and feels good to her even though she is actually just riding the wave of a black woman who has done the work.

Ivanka's brand says it is "committed to helping women create the lives they want to lead." But saying that you stand for and are committed to women and doing things that stand for women are two entirely different things.

The Center for American Progress has posted more than a hundred ways that Trump's policies have negatively impacted women and families. That's more than a hundred times that Ivanka, who serves as special assistant to the president in addition to being his daughter, has had the opportunity to stand up and speak out for women but instead has remained silent.

Trump's policies sought to delay increases in overtime that would have helped women of color greatly, and Ivanka did nothing. They blocked pay transparency protections aimed at ensuring women are being paid fairly, and Ivanka did nothing. They endangered women's retirement security, and Ivanka did nothing. They allowed states to deny women reproductive, educational, and counseling services by limiting Title X availability, and Ivanka did nothing. They attacked Planned Parenthood, and once again, Ivanka did nothing.

At some point, Ivanka must make a decision. Either she is going to stand for women's empowerment, or she is not. Either she is going to stand with women who say "me too" or she is not. Pick a side. Either Ivanka is for women, or she isn't. Her lukewarm performative White Feminism is nauseating. It is an insult to every woman who has stood up and said "me too" for

Ivanka to act as if she's an ally to Oprah and all the women Oprah spoke out about when in fact she is complicit with her silence. It is a slap in the face to every woman who has struggled to tell their story. Most women will never be Ivanka's position. Most women will never be afforded her platform. Most women will never have the opportunity to petition the president for anything on their behalf. And many women who are victimized daily will never have the financial freedom to stand up and say "me too." Ivanka owes it to them to do more than just quote Oprah Winfrey because Oprah is the hot topic today and it sounds good to agree with her.

Oprah stood on the shoulders of women who came before her and spoke for women who are rarely ever heard. "So, I want tonight to express gratitude to all the women who have endured years of abuse and assault because they, like my mother, had children to feed and bills to pay and dreams to pursue. They're the women whose names we'll never know. They are domestic workers and farm workers. They are working in factories, and they work in restaurants, and they're in academia, engineering, medicine, and science. They're part of the world of tech and politics and business. They're our athletes in the Olympics, and they're our soldiers in the military."
Those are the women whose lives Ivanka has the ability to impact. Power and influence aren't given to you to post tweets and do nothing. Use your

power and influence to help those who lack it. Use it for those who life has silenced. Use it for those women who are never seen. That, Ivanka, is how we come together #United as women to change the world. As Martin Luther King Jr. said, "We are caught in an inescapable network of mutuality, tied in a single garment of destiny. Whatever affects one directly, affects all indirectly." There is no way around us. Either we committed to rising together in this movement, or we fail together.

This week, with one self-serving tweet, Ivanka Trump plainly demonstrated the frustrating hypocrisy of White Feminism. She's right that Oprah's speech was "empowering and inspiring," but if she isn't willing to include all women on the pathway to empowerment, liberation, and justice, she would have been better off posting, "Mr. DeMille, I'm ready for my close-up."

HOW NOT TO DO FEMINISM AND INTERSECTIONALITY. I BROUGHT RECEIPTS.
PART I

I am going to present this conversation as much as I can in its entirety, periodically drop in commentary and then follow up.

This is what I wrote in response to Amy Siskind's tweet (who I follow and love reading) about Trump supporting Roy Moore who is an "alleged", pedophile. I was not surprised by Trump's support because Trump is gonna Trump all day. However, I could not sit by and watch White women act surprised by his actions when indeed Trump has not wavered from who he really is as a person. He has shown his true colors time and time again yet for some reason people want to continue to believe that he will somehow be different. I took this time to remind Twitter, because I and many others will NEVER forget, as we are stockpiling can food and water waiting for all hell to break loose, that White women supported and voted for Trump. That one sentence opened a flood of "not all". Listen, I understand why people want to say, "not all" as if that removes them from "those" people. They feel better about themselves when they do not have to look at the totality of their race and wonder how the very people they call family, sit on the PTA with, invite into their homes for tea and cucumber sandwiches could vote for Trump. Acknowledging that fact forces them to look at themselves, to call into question their friends and family and doesn't make it easy to sleep at night. I get it. I understand fully why the "Not All" brigade comes stampeding when the fact is stated that White women voted for Trump. However, like it or not, those are simply the facts. White women voted for Donald Trump and are part of the reason that he is in office. Period.

Now here comes the conversation that I would like to highlight because it shows how NOT to do Feminism and Intersectionality if we want a shot at working together and making this world a better place.

Enter Veronica & Gina in response to my tweet. (I have removed their photos and Twitter names for this publication.)

Hannah Drake
@HannahDrake628

What's over? People knew he was when they voted for him and had no problem with it. When someone shows you who they are, believe them. Remember White women voted for Trump.

4:10 PM - Nov 21, 2017

♡ 266   ♡ 70 people are talking about this

Veronica went on to agree with Gina comments and addressed me about being divisive but NEVER said one word to Gina, about calling me disgraceful and a bigot. Not ONE time did I say anything that was divisive. Facts are not divisive. They are facts. However, calling someone disgraceful, a bigot and an angry Black woman IS divisive. However, you see how Veronica NEVER once said a word about that? She doesn't perceive Gina as the problem, she perceives ME as the problem.

Gina continues...

Hannah Drake
@HannahDrake628

Replying to @HannahDrake628 @GinaMineo65 and 3 others

Stating facts isn't trashing White women. Why do facts bother you so much? It's because you don't want to face reality and THAT is why we are in the situation we are.

10h
Replying to @HannahDrake628 @VeronicaSam13 and 2 others

Whatever you say. I voted for Hillary and so did every white woman I know. We're all educated. Make sure you eat lots of turkey on Thursday.

♡2 ⟲1 ♡1 ✉

Hannah Drake @HannahDrake... · 10h
You are the problem and I am sure when you rest at night you cannot see that. However once your emotion is out of it, go back and read how you addressed me. And check yourself. Not me.

Hannah Drake
@HannahDrake628

Replying to @GinaMineo65 @VeronicaSam13 and 2 others

I never said you didn't however you said I didn't. As well as say I was disgraceful and bigoted as well as tell me to "keep it up" like that was some threat of some kind. Tell me Gina, who do YOU sound like?

11/21/17, 9:12 PM

(When I said, "I never said you didn't", I'm responding to when she said she voted for Hillary)

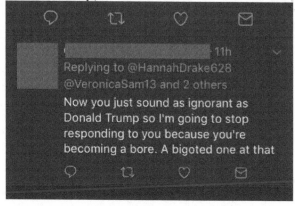

11h

Replying to @HannahDrake628 @VeronicaSam13 and 2 others

Now you just sound as ignorant as Donald Trump so I'm going to stop responding to you because you're becoming a bore. A bigoted one at that

So, let me get this straight. I am disgraceful, a bigot, ignorant and she has made assumptions about who I voted for because I stated a fact. Okay. Let's keep going with this feminism and intersectionality. Those are the buzzwords now, right? It gets better. Keep reading. Now I was done for the night and went to bed. I said what I said and facts are facts. This morning my daughter woke up at 6 am to take our sick dog to the vet. She wanted to be there early because it gets full fast and then you have to wait for hours. Because she didn't know where she was going, I said I would drive her and while waiting I checked my Twitter. However, Gina thinks she is SO important in my life that I stayed up ALL night to talk to her because of course my world centers around her. In fact, my world was focused on my dog. (My dog got medicine and should be fine in a few days.) However, because Gina is SO important in my life and of course is one of the "good" feminist resisting, this is the comment I woke up to. (So it was not ME that was up through the night it was HER. But she cannot see that. She is blind to her own actions. You can see the time stamps. She was up over 11 hours ago responding to me. I was sleeping. Once again, blind.)

Stop with the white women stuff.
Besides every black woman I know
stayed home and didn't bother to vote.
Still a problem white vs black

Hannah Drake @HannahDrake6... ·2h
I'm not going to stop stating facts
because you want me to and it will
make you sleep better at night, Gina.
That's not how this works. You don't
have the luxury of telling this Black
woman what to do.

Hannah Drake @HannahDrake6... ·2h
Your attitude is precisely why we are in
this situation. People that think and act
just like you who do not perceive
themselves as the problem. Stop
focusing on me and focus on you and
your circle. Impact them.

Actually I have the luxury of telling this black woman anything I want. It's called Twitter. You need to get a life clearly you didn't sleep

Hannah Drake @HannahDrake6... · 3m
Gina you are the problem. My life shouldn't be your concern. Focus on you and who you can impact. Try that.

Replying to @HannahDrake628 and @Amy_Siskind

I voted for Hillary. While most black people stayed in bed that day because it wasn't Obama. Delusions of grandeur will get you nowhere.

Hannah Drake @HannahDrake628 · 1h
Gina, facts are facts. The very same thing happened in Virginia and in Alabama there is actually a question if people should support a pedophile or not. I don't need to do any soul searching. I'm not your audience.

Hannah you becoming a bore now so I'm going to do the one thing I love doing. Indifference is the ultimate insult. I'll be ignoring you now.

This conversation continues and you can go to my twitter @hannahdrake628 to see the entire conversation because she continues to respond and the screenshots are endless but I believe as a reader you get the point. To top this conversation off, Gina hit me with the "I am part of the resistance Draw 4 card" the inevitable, "My Best Friend is Black" and doubled down with, "I am raising my child to be 'color-blind'".

Now, I know many of you reading this will wonder, why even engage with someone like this who calls you names and talks down to you? Typically, I do not. However, this time I wanted people to SEE that these are the same women that BELIEVE they have NOTHING in common with the White women that voted for Trump. These are the same women that believe they are not a part of the problem. Not ONE time did I speak to her in an angry manner yet she called me an angry Black woman, a hypocrite, a bigot, disgraceful, angry and old, ignorant, told me she had the RIGHT to tell me anything she wanted and then posted a meme that said, "Deal With It." and to top it off called Black people lazy. But THIS is a woman with her "resistance", "feminism" and "intersectionality" that I am supposed to connect with? How?

This is my PROBLEM WITH WHITE FEMINISM! It is feminism until you tell White women like Gina something they do not want to hear and cannot reconcile and then you are the "Angry Black Woman."

Until women like Gina are willing to look in a mirror, we will continue to have the same problems. Women like Gina do not see themselves as part of the problem and they do not want to do the hard work and self-reflection to change. Women like Gina believe they are perfectly fine. Women like Gina believe they are the "good people". Women like Gina believe they are not like "those people". When it fact they are just two sides of the very same coin. Truthfully, I would take a White woman that tells me to my face, "I just don't like you because you are Black," rather than have a million women around me like Gina, pretending to fight for causes that affect Women of Color, any day of the week. At the very least, I can respect a racist person's honesty. I know where to put people like that. Women like Gina remain hidden in the shadows and it is those that lurk in the lukewarm shadows that are the problem.

UPDATE: Let me say, thank you to those that have read and shared this blog. I had no idea when I was posting on Twitter that this would become one of my most read blogs. I told Gina that I would post this conversation because as she was hurling racist insults at me as an "ally," I saw a teachable moment, which she could not see. For me, that is what matters. I have been called names time and time again, and for the most part, they do not bother me because I understand once people go from facts to personal they have felt attacked. Gina felt personally attacked by the facts. This is obvious when she says her and all her friends that voted for Hillary are educated. No one claimed she wasn't, so that is something internally she holding onto. And so that made it personal for her, and everything Gina ever felt about Black people came out. And I will allow her that. Her facade of resistance was lifted, and her real thoughts about Black women were exposed. However, after she was done calling me names, the fact remains that OF THE WOMEN THAT VOTED, White women voted for Donald Trump. Period.

I never called Gina a name, but Gina blocked me. Blocked the truth. Because when it comes to hearing the truth about these election results and trying to progress, who needs to listen to that? However, MANY White women stepped up and called Gina out on her comments. I applaud them! And not only that, they sent me screenshots of Gina continuing the conversation with me being blocked.

Her comments are a lie. Not one time did I say, "White women are the reason Trump won." However, White women did play an integral part in Trump winning the election. That is a fact. She goes on to call me an "Ignorant woman." (Love that intersectionality!) She also asserts that I "blame ALL White women for Trump." I never said that either. What I said, I posted on this blog, and you can follow me on Twitter to see the entire conversation. Now it may not flow because she blocked me so I do not know if you can read the totality of the conversation, but my words are there. I have no reason to lie about what I said. I do not go to bed in sheets of guilt. I feel fine. Did I love Hillary? No. She had her issues. Did I vote for Hillary? YOU DAMN RIGHT I DID! TRUMP IS TRUMP!

However, Gina and women like Gina are willing to LIE and post comments that will support their narrative. Gina and women like Gina surround themselves with people that support their LIES so they can sleep better at night. Tell me, since this is a White woman that claims she is part the resistance and on my side, how do I stand with a White woman like Gina that is willing to LIE to win an argument on Twitter?

Replying to @RosserClark
@Love_The_Donald and 3 others

Funny I just had an argument with a black woman on Twitter saying that white women are the reason Trump won. Ignorant woman.

#stillwithher

How do I stand with a woman that will block me from responding to her lies so that she can continue to tell her lies with no resistance? How do I stand with a woman like Gina that post comments on Twitter saying "this Black woman," as if that is an insult to me for being Black? How do I stand with Gina and women like Gina that claims their best female friend is Black but in the same breath says, " Every Black woman she knows stayed at home instead of voting" and tells me to get my lazy Black friends out to vote? Gina posts the hashtag #StillWithHer and never once sees me as a part of the "her." Gina and women like Gina exist in their own world of White feminism. They know all the buzzwords to say and post online but when it comes to seeing that in action, I am just one of those "lazy Black people."

It is obvious we still have a lot of work left to do. I thank the women that have stepped up and spoke out and reflected what being an ally honestly looks likes. Thank you. Gina and women like Gina, may not be able to hear me but perhaps working together, they can hear you.

DEAR AMY SISKIND: HOW NOT TO DO FEMINISM AND INTERSECTIONALITY. I BROUGHT RECEIPTS. PART II

Life is indeed a full circle.

November of last year I responded to a tweet written by Amy Siskind, a woman that I follow and that many call an activist and leader in The Resistance.

 Amy Siskind @Amy_Siskind · Nov 21, 2017
Trump just said he is backing a pedophile. It's over.

 Hannah Drake
@HannahDrake628

What's over? People knew he was when they voted for him and had no problem with it. When someone shows you who they are, believe them. Remember White women voted for Trump.

5:10 PM - Nov 21, 2017

♡ 260 ♡ 66 people are talking about this

If you read *How Not To Do Feminism and Inersectionality. I Brought Receipts,* you will see two White women harassed me for hours well into the next day about my stance on the 53% of White women that voted for Trump. Amy never said a word. At the time, I was relatively new to Twitter, and I assumed maybe this is how people who are popular do things. Maybe they turn off notifications for a tweet that gets a lot of attention, and she doesn't see that these two women are harassing me. I have been writing for many years, and as a Black woman I have dealt with White women being hostile towards me, so I didn't need Amy to step in. I felt like I could handle these two women fairly easily. The thought just happened to enter my mind, "I wonder if Amy sees this and why is she silent?" I collected as many screenshots as I could one, because I knew they would block me because people that behave that way always block the truth and two, I knew that I would write a blog about this incident. I am a firm believer that even someone's ignorance can provide a lesson for someone else and as it turns out, my blog was read by thousands of White women that expressed their embarrassment and anger at the two women that were harassing me. I was pleased that even in an ugly situation, there is always room for someone to learn and grow.

That blog article is several months old, and I hadn't given it much, if any thought until yesterday when Amy Siskind's name popped up in my feed along with 2 threads by two Black activits that revealed tweets, articles and videos that did not align with a woman that is billing herself as an activist that works for the safety and opportunity for all women. I read Amy's tweets about her support for Sarah Palin and her dislike of Obama as well as her pulling her support for Black Lives Matter. One tweet called on people to join her to "return America to...by voting out Obama." To what? To when it was White? To when Black people were picking cotton? Return it to what by voting out Obama? **She never states what people would be returning America to, but for her to be a voice of The Resistance, I find it funny that her very words sound precisely like a slogan I have come to loathe. Perhaps she wanted to make America great again.** I repeatedly asked Amy what she meant by her tweet, and she never responded but was sure to reply to and retweet others that did not challenge her. Imagine that?

Hannah Drake
@HannahDrake628

Follow

Replying to @Amy_Siskind

When you made this tweet, what were you implying America be returned to? If I inadvertently overlooked the answer in your blog please point it out.

Amy Siskind ✔
@Amy_Siskind

If Palin runs yes. If it's Santorum, hell no! @rebeccafeldman. Will you join me in 251 days to return America to...by voting out Obama?

2/29/12, 10:15 PM

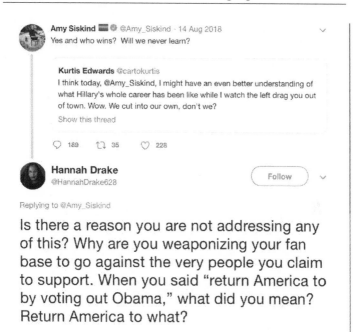

Amy Siskind ☑️ @Amy_Siskind · 14 Aug 2018
Yes and who wins? Will we never learn?

> Kurtis Edwards @cartokurtis
> I think today, @Amy_Siskind, I might have an even better understanding of
> what Hillary's whole career has been like while I watch the left drag you out
> of town. Wow. We cut into our own, don't we?
> Show this thread

♡ 189   ♻ 35   ♡ 228

Hannah Drake
@HannahDrake628   (Follow)

Replying to @Amy_Siskind

Is there a reason you are not addressing any
of this? Why are you weaponizing your fan
base to go against the very people you claim
to support. When you said "return America to
by voting out Obama," what did you mean?
Return America to what?

As I continued reading the threads by the Black
women that brought Amy's comments to light, it
was stunning to see so many White women that
follow Amy and claim to be allies, turn on Black
women and vilify and harass them even to the
extent of being labeled Russian operatives and
being reported to Twitter. In a time where Black
women are carving out spaces to have a voice,
Amy used her fanbase to try to silence Black
women. In a time where Black women are fighting
for air to breathe, Amy remained silent. She
weaponized her followers to take down Black
women because they disagreed with her. Tell me
again about how Amy is an activist? Tell me again

about how Amy fights for intersectionality? Tell me again about Amy working to dismantle oppressive systems? When she did choose to address the issue once she realized it was not going away, did she apologize to the women? No. Did she speak to her followers and tell them don't be like her- when you mess up just own it? Nope. Did she tell her followers to stop harassing them? Of course not. Amy did what White feminists that specialize in White Feminism always do. She wrote a blog on Medium calling it, "My Story…" and in one line summarized up everything that I hate about White Feminism, "**So about me.**"

That's it. So very typical. The rest of the blog is basically Amy talking about Amy.

Amy is the picture of everything I despise about White Feminism and Intersectionality.

1. **White Feminism is never about the people, it always seeks to serve self. White Feminism always centers itself.**

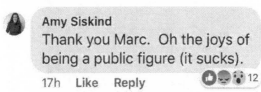

2. **White Feminism is performative. It is manipulative. It aligns itself with marginalized groups only for its benefit.**
3. **White Feminism uses gaslighting**

tactics. **It plays the victim.**

Amy Siskind

Sofia. I am the victim. I was minding my own business - actual taking a 24 hours vacation away and Twitter was lit on fire with old tweets put together to form a false narrative about me. That actually IS being a victim.

1 min   Like   Reply   More

4. White Feminism uses the, "all the Black girls are picking on me" card. It weaponizes White tears.

Amy Siskind For what it's worth to you: I personally prefer you respond to the world around you the way you see fit. I follow you for you, and I follow others for them so I can get some balance. I can imagine how you must have been attacked: I was attacked today through Facebook messenger and accused of not caring about black women and of fawning all over you and ECM – which is nuts - just because I pushed back a teeny bit to some people on the feeds under the posts concerning this issue.

2m   Like   Reply

Amy Siskind

Wow that is just crazy. That is like bullying and a gang mentality - not cool! Thanks for having my back!

1m   Like   Reply

Amy Siskind

I guess I'm confused. When you say exposed, I would call it a smearing. As they had me "dragged" all over Twitter. I don't mean this in a disrespectful way – but I didn't know either of them prior to this - yet the chose to put together a false narrative about me and spread it far and wide when I had done nothing to them. I'll never get it so I won't even ask, but they owe me an apology. What they suggested with their patched together stories is not true and was meant to disparage me (and that worked).

5. White Feminism is dismissive. It fails to

acknowledge or correct past hurts or wrongs.

  Amy Siskind
1 hr · 🌐   ...

In retrospect I'm sure we all have things we wished we had done differently. Keath's comments is how I feel - and I need to now focus on the work. Years and decades from now after the Trump regime is out of power, and we need to reverse the damage done, The Weekly List will be our trail map back. And so now I must focus on listing. Peace out

🙂 **Keath Mayes**
I voted for W. the first time out. I came to regret that. I voted for Obama very reluctantly his first term. I came to love him and very proudly voted for him his second term.

Life is long. Opinions change. What matters is what's happening now.

It doesn't matter who Amy voted for in the past. What matters is her work. Her work is why she's being attacked.

I challenge the real Amy Siskind to please stand up! Are you about resistance and advocating for women's & LGBT rights, & equality, or are you about dismissing Black women that seek to hold you accountable?

Amy understands that using words like diversity

and intersectionality sounds good. It's profitable. Writing a book about resistance is good for business now. Being down with the marginalized groups is cool now. **Everybody has a Black friend**. Resistance is all the rage and **Amy offers the type of resistance White women can align with. Amy provides lemonade, and apple pie type resistance and Black women like me provides collard greens, cornbread, and hot sauce resistance. This ain't your let's sip mimosas and discuss what we are going to write on our protest signs for our Instagram photos while we knit pink pussycat hats type resistance. This ain't my feelings got hurt because you tweeted something that made me uncomfortable, so I quit type resistance. This ain't I expect a gold star and a plate of warm chocolate chip cookies for doing the right thing type resistance. This is can you face some painful truths about yourself, White people, and America type resistance. This is can you understand that as a White person you benefit from systems that oppress Black women type resistance. This is can you go into this knowing it is not always going to feel good but is good for you type resistance. This is can you fight with me and for me because Black women are struggling to breathe type resistance.**

Can you do that?
Or will you take your resistance toys and go home after all this is over? Will you quit because your

feelings are hurt? Will you stop resisting because a Black woman spoke the truth about racism and it made you uncomfortable? Will you refuse to fight because Black women are holding a White "ally" accountable? Will you quit because White people are doing well again? Understand that Black women didn't wake up in November 2016 and realize this nation was racist and oppressive. Some of *you* woke up in November, and the only reason you care about oppression now is because the chickens have come home to roost.

I want to know after Trump is impeached or voted out of office, where do you stand? Do you stand with Black women in hashtags only? Do you stand with Black women as long as we are silent about your favorite White resistor?

Do not write one more hashtag about #TrustBlackWomen, #VoteLikeBlackWomen or #ListenToBlackWomen, if you are not sincere. Instead of checking a heart on Twitter and Instagram, check *your* heart and your motives. It means NOTHING to me if you do not listen to Black women before we are in the fire. Black women TOLD YOU about Donald Trump. Black women told you about Roy Moore. Black women told you about Mike Pence. **It would do you well to bet on Black. Black women are TELLING you about Amy**. When will you listen? I have asked Amy repeatedly to answer the question about "returning America to what, and she doesn't want to answer my question perhaps because she knows the truth and the truth is ugly and makes her uncomfortable.

Newsflash, Amy if you're going to do ANY type of REAL resistance work, it dwells in the realm of being uncomfortable. Amy doesn't get the opportunity to fool me twice. I believe she is exactly what she has shown me and that is why she will avoid my question.

If you read this commentary and want to know how to do feminism and intersectionality, it's simple. Do not be like Amy.

FROM COLLISION TO COLLABORATION-FROM WHITE FEMINISM TO TRUE INTERSECTIONALITY

The Merriam- Webster Dictionary defines the word collision as the coming together of two or more things with such force that both or all are damaged, or their progress is severely impeded.

On the E! Entertainment Golden Globes red carpet Tarana Burke responded about the #metoo movement as she stood next to Michelle Williams, "This moment is so powerful because we're seeing a collision of these two worlds," Then, Burke paused and said, "Collision's probably not the best word. A collaboration between these two worlds that people don't usually see put together and would most likely have us pitted against each other. So, it's really powerful to be on the red carpet tonight."

I believe that Burke actually said the correct word when she said collision. The outcome of the November 2016 election coupled with the sexual harassment epidemic of Hollywood has caused a collision of two or more things colliding with such force that both or all are damaged or their progress severely impeded. With the Women's March and the #MeToo Movement, we have entered a world where two or more things find themselves coming together with such force that we can and have left each other damaged.

Let's just be honest.

We are entering a space where two roads would often never traverse.

We are navigating the road of the Have and the Have Nots, Black and White, Rich and Poor, Hotel Guest Executive and Housekeeper. The differences between us are glaring and overwhelming.

So stark that we never imagined that one day our worlds would collide and that is why we are grappling or as it is defined struggling with or working hard to deal with or overcome.

Let me be transparent and honest. Because in 2018 it's time out for sugar-coating!

After the November election when the rose-colored glasses of so many White women were crushed, as a Black woman, I struggled in accepting White women as part of the movement. I was laser focused on the 53%. I was offended by this newfound dedication for liberation. I couldn't wrap my mind around the fact that Black women have been SCREAMING FOR YEARS and we were IGNORED! I was devastated that in this #metoo movement a Black woman was overlooked for starting the movement. A movement that was started since slavery when White women turned a blind eye and deaf ear to cries of help coming from the slave cabins. I was ANGERED that a White woman could hashtag a movement and it caught fire. Even more UPSET that a White woman could use a movement started by a Black woman to greenlight a reality show. I was INFURIATED that OUR TRUTHS needed to be whitewashed to be heard.

My longing for liberation as a Black woman collided with White women that vowed to stand alongside me that wanted to fight with me.

So how do I begin to reconcile this? How do I start to share my feelings? How do I speak my truth without White women that genuinely want to fight for the cause, feeling offended?

And I decided, I have NO OTHER OPTION but to SPEAK THE TRUTH and ASK MY QUESTIONS that I asked months ago and allow the chips to fall where they may.

Where were you?

Where were you when we screamed for your husbands to stop fucking us and raping our daughters?
Where were you when Recy Taylor was begging for   justice?
Where were you when Anita Hill was vilified for speaking up against sexual harassment?

Where were you when a former officer and

convicted rapist, Daniel Holtzclaw, raped Black women?
Where were you when we buried our sons and daughters?

Where were you when Dajerria Becton had a knee on her back and was assaulted by an officer? Where were you when a young Black girl was thrown across a classroom?

Where were you when Alesia Thomas uttered, "I Can't Breathe", after getting kicked in the throat and groin in the back of a patrol car in 2012, before it became a slogan?

Where where you when Jaquarrius Holland, Ciara McEvleen, Jojo Striker, Keke Collier Mesha Caldwell, Jamie Lee Wounded Arrow and Chyna Dupree were murdered?

Where were you when we marched and shouted for Sandra. Rekia, and Aiyana?

Where were you when we demanded that Black women MATTERED in this fight against police brutality?

Where were you when this nation sterilized Black, Native American and Puerto Rican women without their consent?

Where were you when Michelle Obama was called an ape, evil, ugly?

WHERE WERE YOU?!

I DO NOT want any EXCUSES! I do not want to hear NOT ALL! I do not want to hear NOT ME!

What I want to hear is, "You are RIGHT. AS A WHOLE, WE DID NOTHING! WE USED OUR POWER, PLATFORM, AND PRIVILEGE FOR OURSELVES. WE IGNORED YOU! WE TURNED A BLIND EYE TO YOUR CONCERNS! And if WE ARE HONEST, WE IGNORED YOU BECAUSE YOU ARE BLACK, YOU ARE POOR, YOU'RE THE SECRETARY, YOU'RE JUST THE HELP AND WE DIDN'T CARE. <u>And WE ARE SORRY!</u> We weren't listening to you then but we are here and listening now. We are here working WITH YOU to bring about change. So we will use our privilege and platform, allowing YOUR voice, YOUR needs, YOUR concerns, to lead the way."

THAT is how we MOVE from collision to collaboration.

Will it be easy? NO! IN FACT, COUNT ON IT TO BE DIFFICULT AND MESSY! However, most things that are worthy are never easy! Right now we are STILL in a collision phase-learning, maturing, growing, working towards collaboration. Allow this time of collision. Allow us this space to rub up against each other even if it causes friction. Because it is in the friction that we learn how to SEE, HEAR, UNDERSTAND and FIGHT for each other.

WHY ARE BLACK WOMEN ALWAYS THE CLEAN UP WOMAN?

"I didn't have the luxury of only loving my own children. My own mother, I remember being blue. Blue from the dark of the morning. When the moon would still be up, she kissing me and my sisters on the eyelids, us pretending to be asleep. She going off to work to wake and kiss some other woman's children in the sunlight. I swore that my own children would have all of me. Now I know what my mother must've of known. That is something had ever happened to that other woman's children, that would have been the end of us. Now I know she left us not just out of duty but out of love. Now I know, that love is a kind of survival."

This quote is from the Netflix movie, Mudbound, in which Mary J. Blige, plays Florence, a married Black woman that must leave her own family and take care of Laura's children, a White woman, whose children have have whooping cough. Florence has to "clean up" Laura's mess because she failed to take her children to the doctor when they first started getting sick and now weather doesn't permit them to drive to get medical attention. Florence, who isn't a nurse now must find a way to use her skills as a mother to tend to Laura's family. The failure of Laura to do her part has now somehow created an emergency in Florence's life.

I watched this scene, and my mind keyed on Florence's words, "I didn't have the luxury of only loving my own children." I was reminded of how many Black women had to hold White children to their breasts, feeding and nurturing the children of their slavemaster. Black women are never allowed just to be whole. The world always comes to steal pieces of them, and they are left picking up the fragments of themselves, fashioning them together in some Frankenstein creation, always left quilting together their humanity.

Why must Black women always be the clean up woman?

In the wake of a Sport's Illustrated investigative story that exposed the rampant sexual harassment allegations of the championship Dallas Maverick's, Mark Cuban revealed that a Black woman Cynthia Marshall has been hired as the "interim" CEO. While many people celebrated her appointment on social media, I paused and asked myself, "Why now?" "Why did Mark Cuban hire Cynthia at this moment in time?" Cynthia Marshall is a Black woman that has been honored twice by Black Enterprise as one of the 50 most powerful women in corporate America. Black Enterprise describes Marshall as, "a quick thinker, straight talker, and highly respected leader who was senior vice president, Human Resources, and chief diversity officer at AT&T before she retired in 2017 to launch her own consulting firm." Black Enterprise goes on to say, "A San Francisco Bay area native, Marshall was on a visit to her hometown when her phone rang. It was a former colleague, calling on behalf of Maverick's owner, Mark Cuban, who was eager for the opportunity to speak with her directly. Cuban was facing a crisis, the colleague told her, adding, "You are uniquely positioned to be helpful to him."

Uniquely positioned to be helpful to <u>HIM</u>. Really? Imagine that.

Before I finish this blog, let me say, I believe that Marshall like MANY Black women are HIGHLY qualified; and if I may be honest, even OVER qualified for many positions. So, why do Black women always have to be hired after a scandal, after an incident, after the social media misstep, after the drama, after the crisis?

Why are Black women always called in to clean up the messes?

When I expressed this concern on social media, someone told me, "I just think that you tend to see bad where maybe there was some good. I appreciate that Cuban hired the best person for the job. I hope you don't think he just put her there because of her color and the fact that she's a woman."

In fact, that is precisely what I think.

Do I think Cynthia Marshall is qualified? Undoubtedly. Do I believe Cynthia Marshall will get the job done? Indeed. Cynthia Marshall is more than qualified to right the ship. I do not now nor will I EVER doubt her abilities. Cynthia Marshall was qualified BEFORE the sexual harassment scandal. And that is where my issue lies.

There is this continuous theme in America, and it has happened since Black women were brought to this land. Black women had to sacrifice the very being of who they were in order to clean up the messes of White people. Black women had to pick the cotton, birth her kids, raise her kids, raise the slavemasters kids, be raped by the slavemaster, birth kids that were conceived through rape, cook for the slavemaster's family, take care of her own husband, help the slavemaster's wife give birth, and then breastfeed the slavemaster's children. Black women had to clean up all the messes.

And if and when Black women had a moment to breathe, here comes the world calling. Once they have made a mistake. Once everything has gone to hell. Once everything is turned upside down. Once everything is ruined. Please, Black woman, come fix it. Just give it to a Black woman, she will fix it! I feel like Black women are locked behind one of those cases where people keep the fire extinguisher that reads, "In case of emergency, break glass." Come fix it, Cynthia Marshall, even though I ignored the rampant sexual misconduct in my own organization. Come fix it, Michelle Obama, even though this nation never

COLLECTIVELY stood up for you or your husband in 8 years. Come fix it, Oprah, even though we voted for a reality TV star. Come fix it, Anita Hill, even though we didn't COLLECTIVELY stand up for you as you were battling sexual harassment. Come fix it, Black women, even though we still voted for a racist, alleged pedophile. Come fix it, Black women even though 53% of us voted for a man that was racist and divisive. Come fix it, Black women. Clean up our mess. Let us nurse on your breasts some more.

I KNOW Black women are QUALIFIED. WE KNOW Black women are QUALIFIED. BLACK WOMEN HAVE BEEN, ARE, AND ALWAYS WILL BE QUALIFIED!
IN KNOWING THAT, BLACK WOMEN SHOULD NOT BE AN AFTERTHOUGHT- ONLY CALLED ON ONCE SHIT HITS THE FAN!
Perhaps, just perhaps, Black women wouldn't have to rush in and CLEAN UP YOUR MESSES if you THOUGHT ABOUT BLACK WOMEN AT THE OUTSET! What would this nation and world be, if Black women were considered, BEFORE THE CRISIS? What if you recognized the value of Black women BEFORE you started your so-called "diversity campaign?" How different would the outcome be if you listened to BLACK WOMEN BEFORE YOU VOTED FOR AN ASSHOLE? What could we become if you listened to Black women FIRST and not LAST? If you asked

Black women NOT to be the "interim" CEO but "THE CEO?" What could your organization be if you invited Black women to the table BEFORE the scandal?

We are tired of only being asked to the table so that we can swoop in to clean up your messes. While I know Black women may make this look easy, it ain't easy. We do not have an S on our chests. We are tired of being the afterthought; the Black woman that's looked over until there is an emergency. We are tired of cleaning up your messes. We are tired of being your maid and wet nurse. Black women are qualified from the very beginning, and I am willing to BET if you listened to Black women at the OUTSET, you wouldn't need to call us in to clean up your messes in the end.

DEAR WHITE ALLIES, STOP DANGLING ALLYSHIP IN THE FACE OF BLACK PEOPLE LIKE A CARROT

As someone that spends their life trying to improve the landscape of our humanity, I am always delighted when someone approaches me and tells me that they are an ally. If we desire for this world to be a better place, we will get there much faster if we realize that we can accomplish much more working together than apart. In fact, I am always baffled by people that exist in horrendous conditions that cannot see that it is not us that should be fighting one another, but in fact, our fight should be with the few that seek to keep their power and position by dividing the many.

After the election of Donald Trump, many White people stepped into the arena with Black activists ready to fight, and we welcome them. However, please know, resisting is nothing new for Black people. While you may have had the luxury of enjoying your cucumber sandwiches, afternoon rosé , and hot yoga classes never once bothered by the injustice all around you until November 2016, this is something that many of us live and breathe daily.

So, it is beyond irritating to see a White person that claims to be an ally come online and tell a Black person they may be isolating potential allies when we speak our truth.

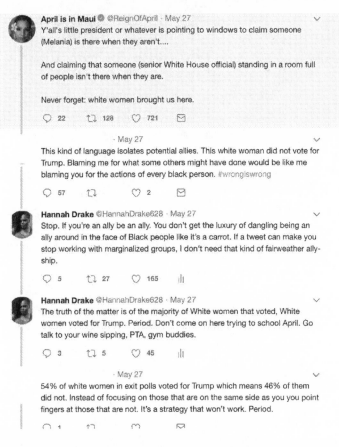

April is in Maui ✓ @ReignOfApril · May 27

Y'all's little president or whatever is pointing to windows to claim someone (Melania) is there when they aren't....

And claiming that someone (senior White House official) standing in a room full of people isn't there when they are.

Never forget: white women brought us here.

💬 22   🔁 128   ♡ 721   ✉

· May 27

This kind of language isolates potential allies. This white woman did not vote for Trump. Blaming me for what some others might have done would be like me blaming you for the actions of every black person. #wrongiswrong

💬 57   🔁   ♡ 2   ✉

Hannah Drake @HannahDrake628 · May 27

Stop. If you're an ally be an ally. You don't get the luxury of dangling being an ally around in the face of Black people like it's a carrot. If a tweet can make you stop working with marginalized groups, I don't need that kind of fairweather ally-ship.

💬 5   🔁 27   ♡ 165   ⫿⫿

Hannah Drake @HannahDrake628 · May 27

The truth of the matter is of the majority of White women that voted, White women voted for Trump. Period. Don't come on here trying to school April. Go talk to your wine sipping, PTA, gym buddies.

💬 3   🔁 5   ♡ 45   ⫿⫿

· May 27

54% of white women in exit polls voted for Trump which means 46% of them did not. Instead of focusing on those that are on the same side as you you point fingers at those that are not. It's a strategy that won't work. Period.

💬 1   🔁   ♡   ✉

When I saw this happen to April Reign, I knew I would have to address this issue because the same thing has happened to me numerous times regarding my blog as if I am sitting at home before I type thinking, "Let me water down the truth so that I do not upset a White person." Trust me, that thought never enters my mind. I am not concerned with your feelings being hurt. I am concerned with the truth. If the truth offends you, I suggest you get thicker skin or bypass my writing. I will never change my message to win over White people. That will not happen today, tomorrow or ever. The truth is simply the truth.

After I made my comments on Twitter, I realized that I was incorrect in my statement. I said she doesn't get the luxury of dangling being an ally in the face of Black people like it's a carrot, but in fact, she does have that luxury. As a White person, she gets the luxury of deciding if she is going to fight for justice. White people get the luxury of weekend protesting as a hobby because protesting is the "in" thing to do. White people get the luxury of reposting tweets and hashtags without doing any of the groundwork. White people get the luxury of serving on panels about diversity and inclusivity, teaching racial bias training, writing the commentaries and being the face and voice of movements they never created or laid the groundwork for. White people get the luxury of going on TV regurgitating talking points Black people have already made on social media for years, yet when they say it, it's celebrated as outstanding wisdom. White people get to decide, "I've had enough of this, and I'm tired. I don't want to do this today." White people get to say, "My feelings were hurt over a tweet, so I am done fighting for justice. I will just go back to my life of convenience."

That is the difference between us. Black people do not have that luxury. We don't have the convenience of quitting because someone tweeted something that made us uncomfortable. Our very breath is connected to us fighting. And you have the unmitigated gall to believe, that before we tweet, we are thinking about not offending White people because they may decide not to be an ally. Newsflash, if your loyalty of standing with Black people can bend like a blade of grass in the wind due to a tweet or blog that discusses the TRUTH, you were never standing with us to begin with.

Many allies became allies on November 9, 2016, when they woke up Wednesday morning and realized, "Oh Trump meant me too." Then suddenly you realized it was time to fight. But before you get to that part, you need to pause, look in the mirror and be honest with yourself about how we got here. Let me be clear, if you call yourself an ally, you don't get to skip over history and the truth to the ally part. You don't get to treat justice like a buffet, casually putting what you want to eat on your plate and bypassing what doesn't look or taste good to you. Like, "Oh I will just get some of the catchy slogans on posters for Instagram pics and one of those pink hats and just hold the Jim Crow and police brutality information." That is not how it works. You need to face some difficult and potentially painful truths, and if you are not ready to do that, you are not prepared to be an ally. Because you are not anchored in anything, but your emotions and emotions waver.

Scrolling through my Twitter feed today I encountered this tweet that has been reposted numerous times.

> @ResistanceParty
> @realDonaldTrump I am a white privileged straight woman. Until this THING is out of office, I am black, I am gay, I am muslim, I am poor, I am trans, I am mexican, I am an immigrant, I am a "me-too" victim, I am a child being held in a cage, I am an American

While I understand what they are trying to say, they have tried and failed. This is racial justice Twitter theatrics. As a Black woman do you think I feel good because a White, privileged, straight, woman is tweeting, she is Black? Do you think that does something for anyone in these groups? And then the post says, UNTIL this Thing meaning Trump is out of office, they are "these people." So what happens after that? What happens after being part of the resistance isn't cool? What happens when you are asked to sacrifice? What happens when your friends don't want to invite you to dinner anymore because of your stance on race? What happens when you read a tweet that challenges you and your feelings are hurt? Then what?

Emotion alone cannot drive allyship. When you are fighting for justice, your feelings will waver. There will be good days, bad days, and days that you feel like throwing in the towel. I can guarantee you that you are going to read something about White people that offends you. If you don't believe me, keep reading through this blog. If you are not anchored in something more profound than your feelings you will threaten to quit. You will treat being an ally like you are dangling a carrot in front of the faces of Black people and if someone posts something you do not like, you can just take your allyship away. If you being an ally is rooted in always feeling good, by all means, do not call yourself an ally of mine. If being an ally is rooted in always reading things that make you want to cuddle up with a cup of hot chocolate, this might not be the role for you. If being an ally means coming on Twitter and telling a Black woman that she might not want to speak her truth because that can isolate potential allies, please do not consider yourself an ally.

In the fight for justice, we do not need fairweather allies, allies that are only loyal on the sunny days. Our struggle is rooted in our very survival. This fight is more significant than a tweet or a blog post or your hurt feelings.

Please do not act like you are doing Black people a favor by standing on the side of righteousness. We are glad that you are here but you are not doing us a favor by doing the RIGHT thing. You should be satisfied doing the RIGHT THING because you SHOULD do the right thing. Be satisfied that you are working to make this world a better place not just for Black people but ALL people and that in itself, should be enough! And if that means you have to be a little uncomfortable for the sake of humanity then so be it! Believe me, Black people have uncomfortable for a very long time.

MANY RESISTERS DON'T WANT CHANGE; THEY WANT TO GET BACK TO BRUNCH

Throughout history, photographs have captured the emotion and message of movements or pivotal times in history. Many of us can recall seeing images that spoke to the times with many of the photographs moving, inspiring, challenging, angering or calling us to action.

I can still recall the emotion I felt seeing former President Barack Obama and First Lady Michelle Obama walk during the inauguration parade.

I was sitting at home having celebratory drinks, holding my breath as he walked down the street waving to the crowd as the first Black President of the United States of America. As a Black woman, I should have been overjoyed, but the image that came to my mind was of Coretta Scott King attending the funeral of her husband, Civil Rights leader, Martin Luther King Jr. as their daughter Bernice placed her head in her lap. This iconic image by Moneta Sleet Jr. would go on to win the Pulitzer Prize for Feature Photography symbolizing the strength, the pain, the heartache and the sacrifice of the Civil Rights Movement.

Coretta Scott King, Bernice King/Photo: Moneta Sleet Jr.

I prayed that Barack Obama would quickly get back into the bulletproof limousine. While many people celebrated that Barack Obama was the first Black President, there was an underlying tension that was boiling up and seemed to spill out November 8, 2016, as America elected Donald Trump to lead the United States of America.

The disbelief and backlash were almost immediate as many people around the country formed bands of resistance to push back against a man that has been openly racist, sexist and divisive.

I recall sitting on my couch as the 2017 Women's March took place, and as a poet my phone was going crazy as people messaged me from all over the country to tune in to watch Ashley Judd deliver her poetic address, Nasty Woman. I watched it for a few minutes, and my soul did not connect with the words that she was speaking. Ashley Judd was saying all the right things, and the audience of predominantly White women in their pink pussycat hats were excited, and hype and shouting as she spoke but nothing on the TV screen resonated with me. I felt confused. I am a woman. I am a mother of a daughter that I have raised to stand up and speak her mind. I am 100% about women having the right to choose. I stand faithfully behind women having the right to equal pay. I am all about women loving who they want to love. I support women that speak out about abuse. Even as a woman that had some fundamental issues with Hillary Clinton when I walked into the voting booth, there was no question about who I would be voting for, yet nothing that came across my screen resonated with me that day. I couldn't figure out why until a photo of Angela Peoples that was taken by Kevin Banatte came across my social media feed. Angela stood in front of 3 White women taking selfies and looking at their phones as Angela stood with a sign that stated, "Don't Forget White Women Voted for Trump," as she nonchalantly sucked a lollipop, in a baseball cap, like the around the way girls L.L. Cool J spoke of in his hit song, Around the Way Girl:

'She can walk with a switch and talk with street slang
I love it when a woman ain't scared to do her thing
Standing at the bus stop sucking on a lollipop
Once she gets pumping its hard to make the hottie stop
She likes to dance to the rap jam
She sweet as brown sugar with the candied yams
Honey coated complexion
Using Camay

Let's hear it for the girl she's from around the way'

Angela Peoples was me. She was authentic. She was unapologetic. She was unfiltered. She was not rehearsed. She was a woman that could be on my block. As L.L. said, she was from around the way. She was a Black woman that understood even in the midst of the hype the reality was that of the White women that voted, 53% of them voted for Donald Trump.

The photograph summed up the disconnect that I was feeling and set the course for where we are today where White women continually stand by and vote for White men that seek to undermine the advancement of humanity in the United States. So apparently, there is a disconnect with the multitude of White women that wear their pink hats and safety pins and the White women that continually show up to vote or perhaps some of them are one in the same because just the appearance of resisting is cool now. Resisting is the in thing. Resisting gives them something to do to occupy their afternoons since soaps aren't that popular. It is cool to wear a RESISTANCE t-shirt and make posters for Instagram photos that might get picked up on national TV. It is profitable for some White women, like Amy Siskind, to RESIST. They are flown all around the world to speak about Donald Trump and the Resistance Movement as they offer their books and resistance merchandise to those that are searching for a way to be a part of something fundamental to impact the world. Resistance is big business for some people.

I recall seeing a Twitter post about The Resistance and how they felt working alongside non-Democrats, and I was appalled. REALLY? Is this where we are now? What DOES IT MATTER if there are people who are NOT DEMOCRATS that understand the fight and want to fight WITH US? Who the hell are these gatekeepers to a movement and who appointed them as gatekeepers?! If you are not fighting against me and want to fight WITH ME, THEN FIGHT! This is not the high school lunchroom where resisting is for the POPULAR KIDS!

However, this is what it is has turned into for many people. For some, it stopped being about Trump and the issues a long time ago and has morphed into likes, retweets, TV shows, books, and spotlights. Resistance has become about popularity and profit and not the purpose.

I am all for people resisting but what happens AFTER the November Election and let's say the Democrats have the majority? Then what?

Then another picture came across my social media feed of a White woman holding a sign that read, "If Hillary was President, We'd Be At Brunch."

That is the reality. Some people are ONLY resisting because THEY have been inconvenienced. It has interrupted their brunch and mimosa hour. Injustice was fine until THEY were inconvenienced. They never noticed racism. They never gave a damn about police brutality. They weren't concerned about other people having healthcare. They never stood side by side with a Black mother whose son was murdered by the police. They didn't care that Black students were expelled from schools at a disproportionate rate. They never cared that Black people weren't getting roles in Hollywood. They didn't care about gun violence as long as it didn't affect them. It didn't matter that Black women were raped by a police officer. No one cared that Trayvon Martin was killed walking home from a convenience store. It didn't matter that Sandra Bland was found dead in a jail cell after a minor traffic stop. No one cared that people threatened to kill Barack Obama. It was okay that Michelle Obama was called an ape. Why? Because their lives were just fine. Injustice didn't affect them. Injustice happened to "those people," not them. They could still go to work and golf, attend hot yoga, their kids were okay, and on Sunday they could have brunch, and all was well. And that is what they want to get back to -their comfort.

Some people are only resisting until they can go back to their normal lives.

You don't want real change you just wanna go back to your brunch.

You don't really care about children being separated from their parents at the border; you just don't wanna hear their cries as you eat your omelet.
You don't really care about police brutality; you just wanna drink your mimosas with no blood on your hands.

You don't really care about feminism and empowering ALL women; you just wanna get back to the days where being a White woman was enough and White women weren't called to task for being silent and complicit.

You don't really care about the 53% and impacting their lives for change; you just want your girlfriend to be able to go to yoga with you without talking about politics.

You don't really care about Black women and representation; you just wanna go see a movie without thinking about all that Black stuff.

You don't really care about racism; you just wanna keep banging your racist boyfriend without feeling guilty.

You don't really care about violence in marginalized communities; you just wanna get afternoon tipsy and be able to go home to your life.

And that is the problem.

Some people want to resist their way back to comfort and not fundamental change. You want to resist your way back to having your head in the sand. You want to resist your way back to pretending racism doesn't exist. You want to resist your way back to a comfortable brunch. You want to resist your way back to when your life wasn't inconvenienced not realizing that for Black people and People of Color our lives our inconvenienced EVERY SINGLE DAY! Our lives don't go back to comfort after an election no matter who takes the House or Senate or Presidency. We don't get to put aside our posters and enjoy brunches with tarragon-infused scrambled eggs, multigrain pancakes, and skinny girl mimosas.

If this election is in the Democrats favor, it is just a moment to breathe, inhale and exhale before Black people and People of Color continue fighting for justice. Because we are wise enough to know our fight didn't begin with an election and it doesn't end with an election.

This resistance will be a continual struggle up a mountain. We are trying to dismantle systems. That is what resistance is. I believe some of you are confused. Resistance isn't how many retweets you can get or how many followers you have. Resistance is not something you do until the next shiny thing comes along. Resistance will be hard work. It will take getting your hands dirty. It will be difficult conversations. It will be long and arduous and disruptive to your day to day existence, and you may miss your Sunday brunch. Just know, we don't resist our way to comfort. We resist our way to change.

DEAR WHITE PEOPLE, BEING AN ALLY IS MORE THAN INVITING A BLACK PERSON TO BRUNCH

It was a typical night on Twitter as I scrolled through memes, funny videos and provocative comments about the impending confirmation of Brett ~~I Love Beer and Sexually Assaulting Women~~ Kavanaugh to the Supreme Court. Make no mistake about it, I was never under the delusion that Kavanaugh would not be confirmed. Even as compelling and truthful as I found Dr. Ford's testimony, I am a Black woman living in this nation and if I know nothing else, I know that White supremacy will always fight to preserve itself. So, I sat back and watched Twitter become enraged as the realization hit that White was going to do what White always does, insulate and protect itself. To be honest, it was interesting after months, even years of speaking about race and injustice, realizing that White people still just do. not. get. it. Too many well-meaning White people are playing checkers while White supremacy is playing chess and Kavanaugh's confirmation was the checkmate heard around the world.

I expected White people to take to Twitter in outrage because that is what people do that have been asleep at the wheel for the past 400 years. They make posts saying, "Oh my goodness I have NEVER seen such injustice in this nation," or "I just ordered a rage pizza, this is no time for a salad" because nothing says let's fight injustice like eating a pepperoni pizza.

The tweets were endless as White people particularly White women felt the safety of being feminine and White being stripped away from them.

And then Bette Midler decided to come online with her loud and wrong tweet.

Bette Midler ✓
@BetteMidler

"Women, are the n-word of the world." Raped, beaten, enslaved, married off, worked like dumb animals; denied education and inheritance; enduring the pain and danger of childbirth and life IN SILENCE for THOUSANDS of years They are the most disrespected creatures on earth.

10/4/18, 7:50 PM

How many times do we have to go over this? Women are not the n*gger of the world. EVER! PERIOD. On a White woman's WORST DAY, she will NEVER be able to understand what it means to be a Black woman. People hightailed it to Bette's tweet to tell us that she was taking the quote from John Lennon and Yoko Ono because of course, that makes it better. If we look beyond John Lennon and Yoko Ono, the loosely quoted phrase can be attributed to Zora Neale Hurston's novel, Their Eyes Were Watching God when she wrote, "De n*gger woman is de mule uh de world so fur as Ah can see." And even if they WERE trying to quite Hurston, she said the BLACK WOMAN was the mule of the world similar to Malcolm X's quote, "The most disrespected woman in America, is the black woman. The most un-protected person in America is the black woman. The most neglected person in America, is the black woman." Lennon and Ono did NOTHING but WHITEWASH the quote and make it something free love, bra burning White women could swallow down. That is the SAME THING Bette did when she got on her ~~Ambien infused~~ Twitter tirade.

After several failed explanations (because you know you can just explain away the n-word) and "apologies," Bette conceded her stupidity and tweeted an apology and stated that she was an ally.

Bette Midler ☑
@BetteMidler

I gather I have offended many by my last tweet. "Women are the...etc" is a quote from Yoko Ono from 1972, which I never forgot. It rang true then, and it rings true today, whether you like it or not. This is not about race, this is about the status of women; THEIR HISTORY.

10/4/18, 10:23 PM

Bette Midler ☑ @BetteMidler · 20m

The too brief investigation of allegations against Kavanaugh infuriated me. Angrily I tweeted w/o thinking my choice of words would be enraging to black women who doubly suffer, both by being women and by being black. I am an ally and stand with you; always have. And I apologize.

◯ 408　　⤶ 340　　♡ 2,406　　

Really Bette? It rings true then and it rings true now? I know every day that I wake up I appreciate allies that haphazardly use the n-word to prove a point. It's funny how many people NEVER want to acknowledge injustice that Black people endure daily but as SOON AS THEY ARE OFFENDED it's "like being a n*gger." You can't have it both ways.

White women this ain't it. It ain't. Why do y'all do this? It's like some of you take 2 steps forward and 3 back every single day.

Many White "allies" Olympic LONG JUMPED over Black women that were explaining to Bette why her tweet was offensive, to tell her her tweet was just fine, because you know, any time I am offended I need a White woman to explain to the world why I am overreacting.

White people that have one Black friend that does their makeup love to claim they are an ally. Having a Black friend doesn't make you an ally. Having a Black person that you sleep with doesn't make you an ally. Having a Black person in your circle that provides you a service does not make you an ally. Inviting a Black person to your brunch where NO OTHER Black people will be present, does not make you an ally. We appoint the label ally. I can dance the choreography to Single Ladies all day long but until Beyonce calls me her dancer, I am a woman dancing Single Ladies in front of a full length mirror in my bedroom. So, fuck your mimosas and basil and thyme infused scrambled eggs. That doesn't make you an ally. What I need to know is, are you willing to go to bat for me? Are you willing to use your privilege for the benefit of others that do not have it?

Are you willing to use your resources on behalf of a Black person, without seeking credit?

Are you willing to stand up and use your voice to diffuse a situation?

Are you willing to advocate for Black people in spaces we aren't in?

Are you willing to tell your husband, your mother, your sister, your brother that their racist jokes aren't funny?

Are you willing to speak up online and say, "That is wrong?"

Are you willing to share an article or blog that may make your friends uncomfortable?

Are you willing to read an article or blog that may make you uncomfortable?

Are you willing to take yourself out of the center?

Are you willing to acknowledge history and how you benefit from the horrors of slavery?

Are you willing to sit through a difficult conversation without saying, "Not all White people?"

Are you willing to demand that Black people be at the table when the topic impacts our lives?

Are you willing to stand with a Black mother that has lost her child to police brutality?

Are you willing to support a Black person even if no one is baking you cookies for doing the right thing?

Are you willing to sit back, be quiet and listen?

Are you willing to let Black people lead?

Are you willing to advocate on behalf of Black women that are paid less and you KNOW they aren't being paid fairly?

Are you willing to step aside so a Black woman that is deserving can have the spotlight?

Or does your self-appointed allyship end by inviting a Black person to an awkward brunch where they are going to be the ONLY Black person, and you think you have done something radical and revolutionary by serving gentrified, grass-fed chicken and gluten-free waffles with agave syrup?

If you be an ally than stand with me, side by side. Be tried by the fire.

I am not impressed by being invited to your brunches or your dinners. I am not impressed being on display for your friends and family members. What impresses me is having the courage to stand up. THAT IS AN ALLY! Someone that is willing to speak up and stand up in the face of opposition.

Are you willing to do that?

If not, please don't call yourself an ally. Just keep swallowing down your mimosas and eating your lox and cream cheese bagel as you watch the world be engulfed in flames.

WHO PROTECTS BLACK WOMEN?

Why you want to fly Blackbird *
You ain't ever gonna fly
Why you want to fly Blackbird
You ain't ever gonna fly
No place big enough for holding all the tears you're
gonna cry

"I know what it like to wanna sing...and have it beat outch'ya." This line was spoken in The Color Purple by the character Miss Sophia played brilliantly by Oprah Winfrey. Miss Sophia was asked by a White woman named Miss Millie if she wanted to be her maid and Miss Sophia replied, "Hell no." That reply was enough for a White man to step in and assault Miss Sophia. What resulted afterward was a vicious attack that not only broke Miss Sophia's body but also broke her spirit. What was once a robust, outspoken woman returned home from spending years in jail, subjected to being Miss Millie's maid, quiet and shattered. It was not until the lead character Ms. Celie stands up against her abusive husband that we catch a glimpse of the former Miss Sophia.

This scene is one that came to my mind after witnessing a White man named Daniel Taylor** assault Yasmine James, a Black woman that was taking his order at McDonald's. Taylor can be seen in the video lunging at Yasmine in what appears to be an attempt to drag her over the counter. In what I assume was, fearing for her safety, James defends herself, hitting Taylor until he releases her, while many of her co-workers simply look on. You would think after watching this man assault Yasmine James, he would immediately be put out of the store. However, that did not happen. From the video, it appears the manager is still trying to serve Taylor. And in fact, Taylor goes on to say, "I want her ass fired right now," as if he has done nothing wrong.

Yasmine yells back to him, "No, you're finna go to jail. You put your hands on me first!"
Taylor responded, "I couldn't control you. I was just asking you a question, bitch!"
And there we have it. "I couldn't control you."
How dare this Black woman deny him what many have said was a simple issue over a straw. And because he couldn't "control her" to him that warranted assaulting her. And still, even that was not enough. It was not until Taylor kicked another female employee in the stomach that he was asked to leave the McDonald's. Why wasn't he asked to leave when he assaulted Yasmine? Was she not enough? How many times would he have to hit Yasmine for it to be enough?

> *'Cause your mama's name was lonely*
> *And your daddy's name was pain*
> *And they call you little sorrow*
> *'Cause you'll never love again*

So why you want to fly Blackbird
You ain't ever gonna fly

Who defends the Black woman? Who speaks out for the Black woman? Who shouts for the Black woman? Who cares about the Black woman? Who says Me Too for the Black woman? Who protects the Black woman?

Over and over again, we have watched countless videos of Black women and girls being assaulted. We have watched Black girls on the ground with the knee of a White man in their backs. We have watched a Black girl thrown across the classroom like a rag doll. We have watched a Black woman assaulted on the floor of WaffleHouse. We have watched our little Black girls murdered with no regard. We have watched a Black woman punched over and over again on the side of a highway. We have witnessed Black women murdered by their lovers. The hashtags of Black women murdered by the police are endless. The names and numbers of Black women and girls that have been raped are astronomical. And this world keeps turning. It never pauses to understand when a Black woman screams for help the earth is trembling.

Who hears us?

Who is weeping for us?

Who is standing with us?

Who shares our stories?

When will our issues be front page news?

When will we stop being props for your election campaigns and marches?

> *You ain't got no one to hold you*
> *You ain't got no one to care*
> *If you'd only understand dear*
> *Nobody wants you anywhere*
> *So why you want to fly Blackbird*
> *You ain't ever gonna fly*

This world demands EVERYTHING from Black women and offers Black women NOTHING in return. And we are tired. We have given everything we can and then some. We have paid debts that we didn't incur with our very lives. We have upheld our end of a bargain that was NEVER for us. We keep waiting and wondering when this world will defend us? When will this world see our value? Are Black women not included in your agenda? Does our plight not sell enough t-shirts and pins and tote bags? Does this incident not fit in with how you define intersectionality? Is the victim not sophisticated enough? Is the victim too Black to fit your agenda? Will she not look good in a pink pussy cat hat? When will you stand up for her and Black women just like her? When will the marches take place for Black women that have been assaulted? When will you shed a tear for Jazmine Barnes, a little Black girl that was murdered? When will this world SEE us? Not just physically see us in an attempt to emulate everything that we are outwardly but when will this nation show us true sawubona- meaning I see you, recognize you, and I connect with your humanity. I understand that I cannot be all that I can be until you are all that you can be. When will that happen? To be honest, I am no longer holding my breath for anyone besides Black women to see me. If you haven't seen us by now, you never will. But I see you, Black women. I see you in all your glory, wonder and splendor. I see you in your beauty and your gentleness. I see you in your love and your passion and even your pain and sorrow. I see you in your intelligence and wisdom. I see you, and I will protect you. Because I want you to sing, blackbird. I want you to fly, blackbird. Because you deserve to soar.

* Blackbird Nina Simone

Conversations Between A Black Woman & A White Woman In A Nation Pretending Not To See Color

A few months ago, I wrote a blog entitled Dear White Women, It's Not You, It's Me. I'm Breaking Up With You. While many White women read the blog, and could not argue with the content, some White women were upset about the article. The blog was shared in the LEO Weekly, a free urban alternative weekly newspaper in Louisville, Kentucky and some White women quickly became defensive and in what I would call typical fashion, made the blog about them and not the totality of what I was saying. I am a firm believer in speaking the truth as well as I can and what most White women did not realize about me is that before I ever take anything back when it comes to speaking out about racism and White people, I will add more to it.

When I started my blog, I understood it would be controversial, and I counted the costs. For me, I had nothing to lose. This was the moment to use my voice, and perhaps I am here for such a time as this. My very first blog, Becky, UGG Boots, and Pussy Cat Hats, reminded this nation that White women had been asleep at the wheel. And while most wanted to quibble about not being part of the 53% eventually some begin to see and you heard words like inclusion and intersectionality being sprinkled throughout talks on race relations in America.

Still, White women floundered. When it seemed as if we took 2 steps forward inevitably, we took 10 more back. And the constant writing and posting about White women was draining at best, especially when time and time again, election after election it seemed they just didn't get it. Or they got it but didn't really care. Their concern for Black women was performative and merely allowed them a way to have interesting afternoon conversations over moscato with their friends. Black women were just a way to pass the time. For every hashtag White women shared about Trust Black Women and Let Black Women Lead, it seems we never could quite find our rhythm. I wrote the blog in such a way that I knew it would cut and I wanted it to cut. Sometimes a surgeon has cut you to heal you. I do not make any apologies for how I write, and I will never be concerned about a White person being uncomfortable when they read my blog. In fact, if you are not uncomfortable, I have not done my job.

~~~~~~

Rani Whitehead

A few days ago on Facebook, I was tagged in a post by Rani Whitehead. Her post is below, and I have copied it in its entirety. I believe this conversation was more significant than me responding to her on Facebook and I wanted to share it with my readers so they can see two women have a conversation about race.

"A few weeks ago I started paying closer attention to the posts and poetry by the black, female poet Hannah Drake. She is a beyond important activist for the black community and she does not hold back, her words cut to the quick and she is not interested in staying on the surface, she goes straight to the bottom and drags up the mess that we have been ignoring or blind to.

When I first started paying closer attention I found myself getting upset, thinking wow this doesn't pertain to me, this is reverse racism, and I am not THAT kind of white person. I wanted to be recognized for being a different kind of white. It became about me. I almost stopped reading. I told myself, Rani, you are uncomfortable, that means there is growth here. Pay attention and LEARN. I speak out often to misogyny, sexual abuse, domestic violence, the patriarchy and I am not interested in staying on the surface, it is the underbelly of vile behavior that needs a beating, it needs to be brought up into the light. That is where I like to focus.

I thought, how Hannah is saying what she is saying is no different than how I like to speak out about the blatant mistreatment of women in our culture but, what is different for me is that I felt attacked. That was what finally got me. Why do I feel attacked? Why do I feel uncomfortable? I SAT DOWN and SHUT UP. I needed to pay attention to Hannah and learn what racism actually is, where it lives, and be willing to see where it lives in me. I needed to see beyond the obvious. I like to think of myself as NOT racist but, what conditionings do I carry around in me that make those words "I am not racist" null and void? If my conditioning that lives unseen under the surface is racist then me believing I am not racist is a lie. I owe it to myself and to the black community to look at myself in a brutally raw way.

Seeing this was and is HARD BUT, is not as hard as living in a society that chokes out your life, literally and figuratively, every day for years upon years, being beat down, ignored, raped, killed, drugged, and dehumanized. Me learning to look into the bowels of my conditioning and seeing how as a white woman, I carry entitlement and racism is HARD but, it is not as hard as being a black woman trying to not only LIVE but, be SEEN and HEARD every day in a world where the only thing reflected back to you is white. I SAT DOWN and SHUT UP. I am learning how to not be racist in EVERY way. I am learning how to replace my conditionings with real life, with the truth. I am learning how to be a vulnerable white woman and understand that all women have it hard but, as a white woman I don't have it as hard as a black woman and my experience is different.

I am learning that Hannah HAS to write the kick you in the teeth way that she writes because the truth is white people want to HIDE from the truth. White people want to make excuses. White people don't want to look at the underbelly because we are the underbelly. I don't care how racist you think you aren't, dig a little deeper and I guarantee you will hit something that goes bump in the night. I guarantee that you carry entitlement and racism. I want to help so much and often feel helpless because I don't know what to say or do. I feel that I don't have a right to engage when I don't even understand the intricacies of what it means to be white and what it means to be black. What I can do is educate myself. What I can do is listen. What I can do is hold space. What I can do is learn to see my conditionings and work to let them go. What I can do is get uncomfortable with being white. Can you? What I can do is reread this and look for ways in which my white entitlement eeks out and learn from it. What I can do is reread this and look at the WHY behind writing it and learn from that. What I CAN do is SIT DOWN and SHUT UP and keep learning from Hannah Drake. Thank you, Hannah for making this white woman uncomfortable."

~~~~

Hannah L. Drake Photo Credit: Jessie Kriech-Higdon/Kriech-HigdonPhotography

Rani,

I was out of town when I read your message but I pulled over to read it and admittedly I was touched. You never know who is watching you or reading your work and truth be told there are some days I think, "Hannah, why do you even bother?" But there is something on the inside of me that just won't let me quit.

All the things you have listed in your post I have heard a million times.

1 Reverse racism. (By the way this is not a thing.)
2 I am not THAT kind of White person.
3 I want to be recognized for NOT being that "kind of White person.
4 I feel attacked.
5 I feel uncomfortable.

The list keeps going and going. However, what is different about you and some other readers is that many people stop at the, "I feel uncomfortable" part. When someone feels uncomfortable, their first instinct is to alleviate the discomfort. I remember when I first started running my shins hurt so bad to the point of tears. I tried to buy every shoe or item that promised to help alleviate the pain of the shin splints. Nothing worked. And finally, it dawned on me, "Hannah, the way to alleviate the discomfort is by going through it." And it wasn't just one day, and I would feel better, but it was a daily process of fighting through the pain and continuing to push through even when I wanted to quit. There were days when everything on the inside of me was saying, "Hannah all you

need to do is sit down, and the pain will be gone."
And that is true. But what would that benefit my
health and my body? I was going to have to fight
through the discomfort and the pain. And one day,
I can't tell you when it happened Rani, but one day
it didn't hurt so badly. And the next day it hurt
even less. And when new people would join the
workout group I could see them suffering, but it
was my job, because I had fought through the pain
to show them there is a way to get through this
and it will not feel good. I do not have a magical
potion. It's going to hurt. But if you can fight
through the discomfort now, you will come out
better on the other side.

That is how I view reading my blog. Go into it
KNOWING this is not going to feel good. This is
going to challenge me to go deep and see all the
ugly in me that I tried to dress up with donations
to Black organizations and claims of being
colorblind. This is going to make me look at
myself, my husband, my wife, my partner, my
lover, my children, my father, my mother
differently. This is going to make me see myself
differently because I thought I was not like the tiki
torch racists. But racism is just racism there is no
racist lite, Rani. Being kinda racist is like being
kinda pregnant you either are or you are not. And
many people have racist thoughts they have never
said out loud that is why a man like Liam Neeson
that seems relatively quiet, hasn't been in the news
before with any scandals or racist tirades, can

casually be in an interview and basically say, I was looking to harm a "Black bastard" because a Black man raped his friend. Now it would be ONE THING to say, I want to harm THAT MAN-the actual perpetrator. I am not going to pretend any of us are above wanting revenge no matter the race when someone harms someone we love. But to say he went out looking for ANY Black man shows somewhere deep on the inside of him, he is racist. And he cannot see that. He thought what he said was just fine. He is not doing the work to acknowledge that he needs to look deeper inside of himself and not just excuse it away. And most people don't want to do that. Why? Because it doesn't feel good. Because it goes against them being "not those White people." And it is easier to disregard my blog or send me an email and tell me "my feelings were hurt," then it is to do what you did.

See it is not the KKK, tiki torch waving White people that concern me so to speak. They are CLEAR on who they are and what they stand for. They don't like me because I am Black. Period. There is no guessing. No wondering. But it's the people that genuinely believe they are "not those White people," that is the problem. It is the "not those White people," that are afraid to fight through their discomfort and I am glad that you did. And you came out on the other side of your discomfort a better person, one that is willing to see herself and challenge others to do that same.

AND THAT, Rani, is why I do what I do and if I have to write it in a "kick you in the teeth" way, I will do just that for the end result to be justice.

I am glad we had this conversation and thank you for allowing me to share it. I believe it will help continue the conversation about race in America. Fight on!

-Hannah

Rani can be followed on Facebook at this link and follow her on Instagram @raniwhitehead

DEAR ALYSSA, WHEN IT COMES TO BEING AN ALLY, TWO COATS OF PAINT ARE BETTER THAN ONE

A few years ago, I was having my bedroom remodeled. I was getting a room with walk-in closets and a full bathroom, and I could not wait until it was completed. Every day I would rush home excited to see the progress and admittedly anxious to get inside of my room. Finally, the day came when the contractor said I could step inside the room and when I walked in everything looked beautiful. I begin to thank him for his work, and he said, "We are not finished. We will be back tomorrow to add a second coat of paint to the walls." In my naivety and rush to be inside my room, I thought the space was complete, and he said, "Oh no, Hannah. Two coats of paint are always better than one."

This interaction came to mind when I read Alyssa Milano's response to a person that asked her was she transgender after she made a tweet that said, "My transgender sisters! I am celebrating you this #NationalWomensDay!" Alyssa response to the question, "Are you transgender," was "I'm trans. I'm a person of color. I'm an immigrant. I'm a lesbian. I'm a gay man. I'm the disabled. I'm everything. And so are you, Kirk. Don't be afraid of what you don't know or understand. No one wants to hurt you. We are all just looking for our happily ever after." Then she followed her tweet with a line from a poem by Rumi, "This is a subtle truth. Whatever you love, you are."

When I read Alyssa's tweet, I had to pause. Surely, we were not going through this again. Understand, it was just in late December of 2017 that Alyssa did the exact same thing with Langston Hughes poem, Let America Be America Again. In her posting of the poem, she highlights a stanza by Hughes forgetting the central focus of the poem that Hughes places in parentheses, America never was America to me, almost as if he wants to draw particular attention to that part of the poem. By cherry picking the part that she wanted to highlight, she missed the entire point of the poem. Hughes is not merely writing about the greatness and tremendous potential of America. However, Hughes is writing about two things in extreme juxtaposition to draw a glaring difference in what America says it is and the reality of what America truly is for Black people.

I wrote about this topic in a blog titled Dear Alyssa, Please Stop With Your Performative Twitter Social Justice. To my surprise, Alyssa shared the blog on her Twitter feed.

MaeQuez and 5 others liked

Alyssa Milano ✔ @Alyssa_Milano · 28 Dec 2017
Replying to @HannahDrake628

Retweeted to amplify your voice. I hear you and now whoever follows me
hopefully will as well. It's never my intention to be anything but light in the fight
for equality.

○ 24   ⬭ 14   ♡ 392   ✉

I took quite a bit of heat from some of Alyssa's followers for that blog, but I felt confident that I was saying the right thing. I believed that Alyssa and I had an understanding and she recognized that what she had done was incorrect. We even started following each other on Twitter.

As someone that considers herself an ally I believed that Alyssa was open to hearing my opinion and in fact we chatted on Twitter and emailed one another and had an open, honest dialogue. I am not above working with anyone that has a misstep. That is part of life. As we are learning to navigate a world that is fueled by differences, there will be some mistakes made. I believe in the quest for justice and liberation there is room for making mistakes and correction.

So, to read her recent Twitter post was disturbing. Did Alyssa not understand my initial blog? When she said that she was sharing to amplify my voice, was that for show? When she said she saw me and was listening, was that a lie? How can she not understand as someone that considers themselves an ally to say that she is transgender, or a gay man or disabled, etc. is wrong? Oh no, Alyssa, that is not how allyship works. You are not the things that you listed. Can you be supportive? Yes. Can you stand with someone that is transgender? Indeed. Can you empathize with the issues that Black people face? Sure. Can you use your platform to bring awareness to problems that disabled people face? Of course. Are you those things? No, you are not. You don't just get to put on these groups like an haute couture gown and take it off when it no longer suits your agenda. I don't ever get to take off my skin. I don't get to wake up and say, "Today I am not going to be Black." Every day that I awake, I am aware of my skin color. In fact, my skin color alone can be the deciding factor in whether I live or die on any given day. My skin is not a costume for me. My skin is my reality. So to tweet that you are those things and then once again back your tweet by a cherry-picked line from a poem written by Rumi is an insult.

Rumi's complete poem states:

If you want money more than anything, you will be bought and sold.

If you have a greed for food, you will become a loaf of bread.

This is a subtle truth. Whatever you love, you are. Rumi's poem has a much deeper meaning and is certainly not saying because I love disabled people, then I too am disabled. It is not saying because I love Black people and People of Color, I too am Black and People of Color. It is not saying because I love transgender individuals, I too am transgender. He is writing a poem that invokes the reader to search their heart. What you love and chase after will consume you and you too, will become that thing so seek and chase after the good things. Not things that are temporal but things that have longevity. Seek goodness, kindness, love, and peace. Love those things so that you can become those things. It is a poem that requires the reader to search inside of themselves and question what are the things that they love because that is what they will become. Alyssa's interpretation of this poem is basic at best and an insult at worst. She would have been better off merely posting the poem and asking her followers to search their hearts when it comes to transgender issues and problems of racism and disabilities. She could have used the complete poem to challenge her readers to examine themselves. The poem reminds me of the Biblical Psalm 139:23-24, "Search me, God, and know my heart; test me and know my anxious thoughts. See if there is any offensive way in me, and lead me in the way everlasting."

Rumi is challenging the reader to search themselves. When it comes to dealing with issues of racism, homophobia, discrimination against people with disabilities, hatred against transgender individuals, a part of the work is to get people to look inside of themselves, to ask themselves the hard questions and then be able to be honest with the answers that are revealed. Why do I hate Black people? Why am I upset that two people love differently than I do? Why am I discriminating against disabled people? Why do transgender people make me uncomfortable? That is how you start to change things when people stop looking outwardly and start looking inwardly. If you consider yourself an ally, Alyssa that is part of your work. How can you get people that refuse to see someone like me and that refuse to see themselves to acknowledge they have some issues they need to address?

Alyssa's tweet caused an uproar online, and since we have been here before, I was once again foolish enough to believe that surely, she would say, "I did it again. I apologize." Instead Alyssa posts a series of tweets excusing her behavior, and in fact, her comments almost read like, "I've been good to you people." Alyssa stated on Twitter, "I learned it doesn't matter how pure your intentions are, or your 30 yrs of advocacy work & activism, if you use well established poetic license & nuance the very people you passionately fight for will be upset because you didn't say it the literal way they'd prefer."

It dawned on me that as helpful as Alyssa wants to be as an ally, she has not done the inner foundational work to search inside of herself and that is why we are here again. Alyssa was catapulted to "Twitter Social Activism Stardom" after sharing the hashtag #MeToo to bring awareness to people that have been victims of sexual harassment and assault. However, the "Me Too" movement was started by a Black woman named Tarana Burke over a decade ago.

In her quick rise in social justice circles, her continuous missteps show me that Alyssa has no foundation on which to stand when it comes to being an ally. Her activism is a house of cards built on sand. It is easy to commandeer someone else's movement as your own. It is easy to go online when you have a vast platform and post something that "sounds" progressive and get thousands of likes and retweets. It is easy to comb through poems and pick a line or two that may help undergird your tweets. It's easy to dress up in a handmaid's costume and not see how your real life actions are not indicative of supporting all women. It's convenient to post a Martin Luther King quote that makes you feel good. It is easy to do all of those things without doing any of the real work. Moreover, the real work doesn't start on Twitter. It doesn't start with a pink pussy cat hat. It doesn't start with some catchy sign held up at a protest. I dare say it doesn't even start with a hashtag. The real work begins when you first look inside yourself and challenge yourself to be better, to do better and to do something.

My challenge once again to Alyssa, if you want to be an ally, do not start with anyone else until you start with yourself first. As I stated at the beginning of this blog, two coats of paint are better than one. This is the second coat of paint, Alyssa. I hope it sticks this time.

#TrustBlackWomen Often Means #UseBlackWomen

Over the past few days, many Presidential candidates have spoken eloquently about Black women and our strength, power, and abilities. As I thumbed through my Twitter feed, I came upon Elizabeth Warren's tweet that had a new plan to address issues that are impacting Black women. I also came across a video of Presidential hopeful Pete Buttigieg stating, "I stand here aware, that Black women are not just the backbone of the Democratic Party but the bone and sinew that is making our democracy whole. When Black women mobilize, outcomes change. "
Thank you, Pete, for that information.

However, newsflash to Pete and anyone else that wants to echo his sentiments...you are not telling Black women anything that we do not already know. And here's the kicker, we KNOW that you KNOW and have always KNOWN the power, influence, and impact of Black women which is why throughout history, White America has either tried to silence it, kill it, or commandeer it -which is where we are now in America.

Right now, we are in awakening where people see the power and potential of harnessing the talent, creativity, ingenuity of Black Women not because they have any real interest in uplifting Black women but because the influence of Black Women is now a commodity. The influence of Black women can make or break an election. The influence of Black women can cause your products to fly off the shelves. The influence of Black women can shift industry standards. The influence of Black women can impact an entire economy. The influence of Black women sets the trends.

Before it was convenient just to hijack and co-opt everything about Black women. Why actually get a "real" Black woman when you can take a White woman and surgically enhance her until she "looks the part?" So, they snatched everything- our hairstyles, our skin color, our lips, our hips, our slang, our mannerisms, our food. Some of them have built entire empires co-opting the essence of Black women. But the funny thing is, no matter how you attempt to co-opt Black women, imitations will never be as great as the real thing.

And this world noticed the shift. So now it is socially acceptable and profitable to pull Black women from the kitchen to the spotlight. It is now cool that a Black woman is your bestie. It is seen as progressive to say you watch Joy Reid and love April Ryan. It is catchy to call Congresswoman Maxine Waters, "Auntie Maxine." It is all the rage now to get in formation. It is acceptable to invite the Black woman to your brunch. It is seen as progressive to have a Black woman on staff. And it's always punctuated with the selling and talking point, #TrustBlackWomen.

For me, that hashtag has become as common as #Diversity and #Inclusion. Those words are stamped on to everything because diversity and inclusion are good for business. However, when I see these hashtags, my first question is, "What is your motive?"

It is easy to create a hashtag and never do one thing to practice diversity and inclusion truly. (I understand that some of the Democratic candidates have some Black women in leadership roles however this extends far beyond any political campaign.) It is easy to say Trust Black Women and NEVER do anything to show that you actually do Trust Black Women. I do not get excited when I hear White people say Trust Black Women. As a Black woman, I understand this phrase in practice often translates to use Black women, allow Black women to do all the work, allow Black women to be the feet and never the face of movements, steal from Black women, harness Black women's ideas and creativity for White America's gain, pay Black women less than their worth, never promote Black women, allow Black women to lead from the back of the line, step on a Black woman's back to get to the top.

Trusting Black Women is more than a catchy hashtag. It is more than a talking point on the campaign trail. Trusting Black Women is more than inviting a Black woman to the table without any leadership or decision-making authority. Do not invite me to the table if I am expected to sit pretty and poised with no power. Do not invite me to the table if you want a sassy, finger snapping, Black woman for entertainment purposes only. Do not invite me to the table so I can be the face of your faux Trust Black Women campaign. Making a hashtag does absolutely nothing without clear motives and actions behind it.

Trusting Black Women isn't done so that Black women can carry you on our backs. Trusting Black Women means as a White person, you are willing to fall back, step aside, decrease so that a Black woman may increase. It means giving Black Women their credit. Trust Black Women means paying Black women their worth. Trust Black Women means listening to the issues that impact Black women and swallowing down the need to say, "Not All." Trust Black Women means owning your part in a system that has been designed to benefit White people. Trust Black Women means allowing Black women to lead with authority. Trust Black women means being a real ally and having difficult conversations with your family members. Trust Black Women means not tone policing Black women because we have said something about racism that made you uncomfortable. Trust Black Women means standing with Black women in our times of need. Trust Black Women means reevaluating and tearing down every single system in America that has benefited White people. Trust Black Women means listening to Black women at the beginning, and not after all hell has broken loose.

If you want to Trust Black Women move beyond making this sentiment a social media hashtag for your gain but make it something that you practice in your everyday life. Only then will things truly begin to change.

Trust me. I'm a Black Woman.

BLACK WOMEN DO NOT OWE THIS WORLD SHIT

Hannah Drake @HannahDrake6... · 8m ⌄
"Your country needs you." Of course saving the country falls of the back of a Black woman. Black women do not exist to save you.

Laurence Tribe ✔ @tribelaw · 5h
.@staceyabrams: Please rethink your decision to rule out a Senate run. Think about RBG. If the Senate doesn't flip, darkness falls. Your country needs you.

Once again, Black Women are being tasked to save the country. You would have to be hiding underneath a rock not to notice the brilliance of Stacey Abrams. It seems everywhere you turn this nation is speaking about her brilliance. But here is the thing, Stacey Abrams was brilliant BEFORE this nation so desperately needed her. She was brilliant when Georgia's gubernatorial election was STOLEN from her. She was brilliant as a community organizer. Stacey Abrams is brilliant because she is Black Excellence.

But in typical fashion, this nation didn't notice her brilliance until they NEEDED HER FOR SOMETHING! Which is typical when it comes to Black Women. White America overlooks Black women until White America NEEDS something. And after they get it, rest assured, Black women will be discarded yet again.

Black women are overlooked and regulated to the back burner until White America says, "Look,

White People, it's a bird, it's a plane. No! It's a Black Woman coming to save us!"

Let me be clear...Black Women Do Not Owe This World Shit!

NOT. ONE.THING.

It takes a lot of White audacity even to ask a Black woman to step up and save this nation. This nation that enslaved Black woman. This nation that raped Black women. This nation that committed medical malpractice against Black women. This nation that mutilated Black women. This nation that murdered our husbands. This nation that kills our children with impunity. This nation that co-opts anything a Black woman does and pawns it off as their own. This nation that ridicules Black women. This nation that mocks our appearance. This nation that despises our hair. This nation that called us "crack mommas" and didn't give a damn about giving us treatment. This nation that labels us, "The Angry Black Woman" for having the nerve to have feelings. This nation that refuses to pay Black women our worth. This nation that incarcerates Black women at an alarming rate. This nation that overlooks the medical needs of Black women. This nation that continuously turns its back on Black women.

And still, this nation has the unmitigated gall, the White audacity to ask Black women to save it from itself. Right after spitting in our faces election after election.

Not today! And tomorrow ain't looking good either!
Black women have paid our dues in blood.
Black women are tired of cleaning up your messes!
Black women will no longer let you suck at the bosom of our brilliance.
Black women are not this nation's mammy. Our titties are tired!

If you want to save this nation, take a long hard look in the mirror. Do not ask us to save you.

Stop asking Black women to swoop in and save this nation. Black women only make this look easy. We are tired. Overworked. Underpaid and highly disrespected. This world treats Black Women like an ATM always coming to us for withdrawals and very rarely if ever depositing anything of any value back into who we are. We aren't playing wetnurse because of mistakes y'all made. Here is a thought, support Black Women doing whatever the hell Black Women want to do and in turn that will bless this nation. That's the

part this nation fails to see; when Black women rise, EVERYONE rises!
But that's too radical of a thought, huh?

YOU BETTER SMILE FOR US, BLACK GIRL.

Fix it, Black Girl. Fix us, Black Girl. Nurse us, Black Girl. Teach us, Black Girl. Be the help, Black Girl. Clean up our messes, Black Girl. Vote for us, Black Girl. Don't complain, Black Girl.

Let us touch your hair, Black Girl. It ain't pretty unless we say it's pretty, Black Girl. Give us your culture, Black Girl. Even better, we will just steal it, Black Girl. Watch us flip it and become rich, Black Girl. Let us kill your sons and daughters, Black Girl. Don't you dare say a word about it, Black Girl. Who fights for you, Black Girl? Who will mourn for you, Black Girl?

You better smile for us, Black Girl. Don't speak unless spoken to, Black Girl. Don't make demands, Black Girl. Your presence makes me uncomfortable, Black Girl. Why are you so angry, Black Girl?

Ignore your health, Black Girl. Put your life on the back burner, Black Girl. Help me fulfil my dreams, Black Girl. Stop taking up so much space, Black Girl. Be all things to all of us, Black Girl. Educate yourself on who we are, Black Girl. Be our cheerleader, Black Girl. Teach us not to hate you, Black Girl.

Labor for our benefit, Black Girl. Let us tear it down and you rebuild it, Black Girl. Sweat for us, Black Girl. Dance for us, Black Girl. Be Venus

Hottentot for us, Black Girl. Let us rape you, Black Girl. Who's gonna believe you anyway, Black Girl? Sing pretty for us, Black Girl. Entertain us, Black Girl. Build movements and let us steal them, Black Girl. Let us co-opt your excellence, Black Girl. Just be satisfied, Black Girl. Give us your ideas for our profit, Black Girl.

Work for free, Black Girl. Stay in your place, Black Girl. We saved you a seat in the back, Black Girl. You should be thankful to be in the room, Black Girl.

Move over, Black Girl.

Minimize, Black Girl.

Shrink, Black Girl.

Disappear, Black Girl.

Don't be so loud, Black Girl.

Whisper, Black Girl.

Just shut up, Black Girl.

Ain't you tired, Black Girl?

BECOME BLACK GIRL.

I see you, Black Girl. Find yourself, Black Girl. Know your worth, Black Girl. Don't settle, Black Girl. Breathe, Black Girl. Take care of yourself, Black Girl. Own your dopeness, Black Girl. Put yourself first, Black Girl. Love yourself, Black Girl.

Dance in the rain, Black Girl. Embrace your body, Black Girl. Cry, Black Girl. You don't have to be strong all the time, Black Girl. Rest, Black Girl. Own your creativity, Black Girl. You are beautiful, Black Girl. Cherish all hues of you, Black Girl.

You've always been enough, Black Girl. Love who you desire, Black Girl. Don't let them use you, Black Girl. Stand in your truth, Black Girl. I believe you, Black Girl. I believe in you, Black Girl. Trust yourself, Black Girl.

Stand upright, Black Girl. Head held high, Black Girl. Be a champion for yourself, Black Girl. You are loved, Black Girl. Be patient with yourself, Black Girl. Take up space, Black Girl. Sing your song, Black Girl. Ride the wind, Black Girl. Soar, Black Girl.

Be Loud, Black Girl.

Laugh, Black Girl.

Love, Black Girl.

Grow, Black Girl.

Dream, Black Girl.

Live, Black Girl.

Become, Black Girl.

DEAR WHITE WOMEN, IT'S NOT YOU, IT'S ME. I'M BREAKING UP WITH YOU!

Dear White Women,

I have thought about writing this letter for years and have finally realized that it is time. Perhaps a letter that has been long overdue. I have spent more than half of my life writing everything from poetry to novels trying to speak to women and encourage women to live their best lives. I knew after the 2016 Presidential election, I had a lot more to say than what could fit in a poem, so I started my blog. My very first blog, Becky, UGG Boots and Pussy Cat Hats, was read by thousands of White women, many of whom challenged me yet ultimately agreed with me and promised to work harder to fight against racism.

I am always one to give someone the benefit of the doubt.

So begin our awkward relationship. We tried to dance but never seemed to be able to catch our rhythm. You seemed to always step on my toes with "Not All" and "Not Me," at inappropriate times. You accused me of being angry and even being racist when I was just telling the truth. Still, I stayed. Even when I started to let my guard down, you reminded me election after election that I was a fool. Yet, you told me that we were in this fight together. So, when it was time to stand up for Botham Jean, a young Black man killed in his own apartment by a White female officer, I looked for you to stand with Black women in protest and I couldn't find you. I looked for you to stand up in the wake of a hate crime in Kentucky where 2 Black people, Maurice Stallard and Vickie Jones lost their lives, only to be met with indifference. Once again, Black women were alone with our tears, pain, quiet suffering and your deafening silence.

But you told me that were in this together. We were part of "The Resistance." Yet daily there were missteps and mistakes from #BBQBecky to Blackface, and still, as Black women, we continued to give you the benefit of the doubt. Today, I feel foolish for believing.

I wrote blog after blog hoping that something would resonate with White women and we would see substantial change across this nation, and it never happened. After this week's midterm election results in key states, I realized that our relationship was never one based in love and understanding. You did not love me or see me as your equal, and throughout history you never did. You were never going to vote for a candidate that fully supported Black women. You were never going to collectively vote against Whiteness. Black women were just your mascot; that Black woman you could point to and say, "Look, I follow

Hannah online, and I read her blog every day and I always like her posts. I am not like THOSE White women. Hannah and I have a relationship." But let's be honest, we don't have a relationship. A relationship is based on trust and mutual respect. And time and time again you have shown me that as a Black woman, I cannot trust you and by the way that you vote, you do not love or respect me. You whisper sweet nothings of justice in my ear. You use words like intersectionality and inclusivity, but you are double-tongued. You say one thing yet repeatedly do another. You have been duplicitous in your ways.

I realized that Black women were just your plaything, something to entertain you on Twitter and Facebook. We were your live and in color resistance rom-com Black best friend. We were your "hey, girl," "yaassssssss," and high fives. We were your sassy finger snap, neck roll, and "Auntie." We were the face of your resistance memes as we "reclaimed our time." Black women made the days pass faster until you could get your next Resistance fix. Until the next march, the next hashtag, the next knitted hat, Black women were your entertainment. Black women were your hidden lover. Someone you cherished online, cloaked in the anonymity of social media with no real commitment. God forbid your racist boyfriend or husband knew you were cheating on him with Black women telling the truth. We were your 2 am social justice booty call. After you got what you wanted from us, you would find your way back home to White patriarchy and supremacy, hoping that you didn't smell of your online Black woman resistance lover. Black women were just the trendy thing, and just like Louboutins or bedazzled fanny packs, White women love to possess what is trendy.

To be honest though, perhaps that is our fault. Maybe we overlooked your flaws because ego got in the way. Many Black women had found an unoccupied niche. A platform that had been covered in dust and cobwebs was now available for us to brush off and assume our seat on panels and nightly news channels underneath glowing lights and hot mics. For many Black women, the period after the election was the only time we had a voice, the only time someone would listen to us, the only time that we were the authority. So, we carved out spaces and demanded checks next to our names to signify that we were the official voice of Black women. We started PayPal and Patreon accounts. We were in demand. For once we were the commodity on our terms. Or so we thought. We fought to hold the 53% accountable but accountable to what? Maybe we overlooked reality. We have tried for years to find common ground and work together yet it never seems to work. So it is best that I stop trying.

Breaking up is never easy to do, but I have decided that for those in the 53% and beyond, I must go my own way and you must go yours. As the saying goes, it is not you, it is me. Throughout history up until today, you have always been who you are, and it is MY FAULT for not believing what you showed me. What I want for Black people is liberation and justice. I cannot fight for those things while trying to pull you along. Black women are drowning, and for me to swim, I must cast aside any dead weight. I am sure somehow you will find a way to float. White women always do. I have decided that I do not have the time or energy to make something work that just doesn't seem like it wants to work. Maybe we are trying to force a relationship that was never meant to be. Perhaps we are pointlessly fighting to find similarities that we just do not have. Maybe we just found ways to tolerate each other instead of genuinely understand each other. Maybe we didn't want to see, and I have to be okay with that as I continue on to fight with and stand with others that are genuinely about liberation and justice.

I can no longer fight to make you aware or make you want to convince your friends and family what is right. If the unjustified murder of Black men and women at the hands of those sworn to serve and protect won't do it, I don't know what will. If the countless KKK rallies won't do it, I don't know what will. If a President that calls

Black women low intelligence won't do it, I don't know what will. If the blatant racist attacks against Black political candidates won't do it, I don't know what will. If a Black mother burying her 12-year-old son won't do it, I don't know what will. If the murder of Maurice Stallard and Vickie Jones, two Black people that just stopped for groceries won't do it, I don't know what will. Black women have explained our position in blood. Do with it what you will.

But now I know, in life, some things just cannot be salvaged.

It's Not You, It's Me. I'm breaking up with you!

Sincerely,

A Black Woman

About The Author

Hannah L Drake is a blogger, activist, public speaker, poet, and the author of 10 books. She writes commentary on politics, feminism, and race and her work has been featured in Cosmopolitan Magazine. In 2019 during Super Bowl Sunday, Hannah's poem, "All You Had To Do Was Play The Game, Boy," which addresses the protest by Colin Kaepernick, was shared by film writer, producer and director Ava DuVernay, and then shared by Kaepernick. The poem has been viewed more than two million times. Hannah's commentary on life and challenging others to dream bigger have been recognized by First Lady Michelle Obama. Hannah Drake was featured on the Tom Joyner Morning Show with Jacque Reid to discuss her international movement, Do Not Move Off the Sidewalk, which addresses the power of holding your space. In February 2019, Hannah was selected by the Muhammad Ali Center to be a Daughter of Greatness which features prominent women engaged in social philanthropy, activism, and pursuits of justice. Recently Hannah was selected as one of the Best of the Best in Louisville, Kentucky for her poem Spaces. Hannah's message is thought-provoking and at times challenging, but Hannah believes that it is in the uncomfortable spaces that change can take place. "My sole purpose in writing and speaking is not that I entertain you. I am trying to shake a nation."

Social Media
Facebook: Hannah Drake or Hannah L. Drake (Fan Page)
Twitter and Instagram: @HannahDrake628
Website: www.hannahldrake.com
Blog: www.writesomeshit.com

Made in the USA
Lexington, KY
30 October 2019